SPPU New Syllabus

A Book of

POLITICAL SCIENCE

[INTRODUCTION TO INDIAN CONSTITUTION]

F. Y. B. A. Semester II
New Syllabus as per CBCS Pattern,
June 2019

By

Prof. Dadaram Laxman Khokale
HOD and Assistant Professor,
Department of Political Science,
Modern College of Arts, Science and Commerce, Shivajinagar,
Pune 5.

Prof. Pramod Rajendra Tambe
Assistant Professor & Research Scholar
NET,SET, PhD (Reg.)
Pemraj Sarda college
Ahmednagar.

Prof. Haridas Arjun Jadhav
Assistant Professor,
Department of Political Science,
Modern College of Arts, Science and Commerce, Shivajinagar,
Pune 5.

Prof. Kailas wagh
Assistant Professor,
K. J. Somaiya college, Kopargaon
Ahmednagar
NET, SET.PhD (Reg.)

NIRALI PRAKASHAN
ADVANCEMENT OF KNOWLEDGE

N5145

Introduction to Indian Constitution **ISBN : 978-93-89825-68-8**

First Edition : January 2020

Published by :
NIRALI PRAKASHAN
Abhyudaya Pragati, 1312 Shivaji Nagar,
Off J.M. Road, Pune – 411005,
Phone : 25512336/37/39 Fax : (020) 25511379
Email : niralipune@pragationline.com

www.pragationline.com **info@pragationline.com**

We have great pleasure to present this book on '**Introduction of Indian Constitution**' to the students of F.Y.B.A. Semester II. The authors have sincerely put their efforts to give complete information on the subject as prescribed in the syllabus of June 2019 in a simple manner.

The first chapter discusses the structure, powers and role of the Union Legislature and the state Legislature. The second chapter deals with the Union Executive and state executive. The third chapter includes the Judicial System in India. Finally the fourth chapter discusses the Electoral system in India.

This textbook has been prepared keeping in mind the exact need of the students and syllabus specified by S.P.P.U. Every efforts has been taken to give clear concepts of various terms relating to the subject. We hope that this book will be very useful to the students and also to teachers. Study of this book will help the students to get an idea and understand the subject thoroughly.

We are thankful to the publisher Shri Dineshbhai Furia and Shri Jigneshbhai Furia and the entire staff of Nirali Prakashn specially Mrs. Yojana G. Deshpande, Mrs. Surekha Sannali, Mrs. Sarika Supekar, Ravindra Walodare for the great efforts they have taken to publish this book on time.

All valuable suggestions from the readers of this book are always welcome.

January 2020

All the Best

Authors

❋ ❋ ❋

SYLLABUS

F.Y.B.A. : Semester – II

Introduction to Indian Constitution

1. LEGISLATURE

(a) Union Legislature : Structure, Power and Role

Organisation of the Indian Legislature

Members of the Parliament-Qualifications and Disqualification, Power and Functions of the Parliament

(b) State Legislature : Structure, Power and Role

Composition of the State Legislature

Power and Functions of the State Legislature

State Legislative Council

2. EXECUTIVE

(a) Union Executive, President , Vice President

Prime Minister, Council of Minister

(b) State Executive

Governor, Chief Ministers, Council of Functions

3. INDIAN JUDICIARY SYSTEM

(a) The Supreme Court (Article 124)

(b) High Court

(c) Judicial Review

(d) Judicial Activism

4. ELECTORAL SYSTEM

(a) Election Commission: Composition, Functions and Role

Electoral System in India

Powers and Function of Election Commission

Election Process

(b) Chief Election Commissioner

(c) Electoral Reforms in India

Changes in the Election Process

Evaluation of the Performance of the Election Commission

❋ ❋ ❋

CONTENTS

❋ ❋ ❋

UNIT – 1

LEGISLATURE

SYNOPSIS

1.1 Union Legislature : Structure, Power and Role

- On the day of 26th January, 1950 India, a newly born republic accepted the constitution. For the first time in the history of the continent; India was transformed into a modern institutional, completely parliamentary democracy. Representatives institution is not totally new for India. Around the 6th century BC few Janapadas out of the 16 were of Republican character. Even before that the Rigveda has mentioned few institutions like Sabha and Samiti which are a lot similar to today's modern democratic institutions.
- The decision-making process in a modern democracy involves debates, discussions and majority; it was seen that a similar process was followed in ancient institutions like Sabha and Samiti. Its mentions are found in many ancient texts and symbols like Aatreya Brahmin, Panini's 'Ashtadhyayi', Arthashastra Parampara, Mahabharat, Ancient texts on Ashokastambha and

some contemporary Greek historians' books, some books written by Buddhist and Jain scholars and Manusmriti. Also, many republics existed in the post vedic period. Republic was known as 'Samadha' in India. Literature in 'Pali' language has records of existence of a Republican System in India.

- The institutions like Janapada, Nagar sabha and Gram sabha existed in India as local self governing bodies and their entire functioning was handled by local citizens. There were local programmes and the principle of self governance. Many ancient texts like Arthashastra, Mahabharata and Manusmriti have records that prove the existence of Village unions. Composition of Gram sabha, Gramsangh, Panchayats through elections is a witness of the ancient nature of the Indian political system.
- Democratic institutions like Sabha and Samiti vanished gradually over time, but the rural level Gram sabha, Gram sangh, Panchayats existed throughout the rule of many Hindu or Muslim dynasties. They existed and kept functioning effectively and evolving over time till the arrival of the British in India. Articles 79 to 122 in part 5 of the constitution deal with the organization, composition, duration, officers, procedures, privileges, powers and so on.
- The parliament is the legislative organ of the union government. It occupies a pre-eminent and central position in the Indian democratic political system due to adoption of the parliamentary form of government also known 'Westminster' model of government. It is described as 'Westminster model of government' after the location of the British parliament near London where the parliamentary system originated. Parliament is the topmost democratic institution to make laws for the governance of the country, and make decisions.
- The main function of its members is to make laws according to the constitution and important policy framework.

1.1.1 Organisation of the Indian Legislature

Structure of Indian Judiciary (Organisation)

President | Rajya Sabha | Lok Sabha

- Under the Article 79 of the constitution, the parliament of India consists of three parts viz, the President, the Council of States and the House of the People. In 1954, the Hindi names 'Rajya Sabha' and 'Lok Sabha' were adopted by the Council of States and House of People respectively. The Rajya Sabha is the upper house, second chamber or House of Elders and the Lok Sabha is the Lower House ,First Chamber or Popular House. The former represents the states and union territories of the Indian Union, while the latter represents the people of India as a whole.

(1) President :

- Though the President of India is not a member of either House of Parliament and does not sit in the Parliament to attend its meetings, he is an integral part of the Parliament. This is because a bill passed by both the Houses of Parliament cannot become a law without the President's assent. He also performs certain functions relating to the proceedings of the Parliament, for example, he summons and prorogues both the Houses, dissolves the Lok Sabha, addresses both the Houses, issues ordinances when they are not in session, and so on.
- Certain types of bills cannot be presented in the Parliament without the recommendation of the President and cannot be processed further. He appoints a pro-tem Speaker of the Lok Sabha and the executive Chairman of the Rajya Sabha if need be. He summons both the Houses for a joint sitting in case of deadlock between two Houses over some bills. The Annual Budget is presented in the Parliament with the prior permission of the President.
- He puts the reports of the important constitutional bodies in the Parliament for consideration which includes 'Comptroller and Auditor General of India', 'Finance Commission', 'Union Public Service Commission', 'Commission for SCs and STs' and 'Commission' and 'Commission for Other Backward Classes'. The president can nominate 12 members of the Rajya Sabha who have special knowledge and experience in the field of education, literature, science, arts or social sciences.

- These functions performed by the President related to the Parliament make him an integral part of the Parliament. We will study his powers, functions and roles in the detail in the second chapter.

(2) Rajya Sabha :

Composition of the Rajya Sabha : Under the Article 80 of the Constitution, the maximum strength of the Rajya Sabha is fixed at 250, out of which 238 are to be the representatives of the States and Union Territories and 12 are nominated by the President. Members of the Rajya Sabha are elected indirectly from the states on the basis of proportional representation from the State legislative assemblies by the method of single transferable vote. All the States and Union Territories don't have equal representation in the Rajya Sabha. The Fourth Schedule of the Constitution deals with the allocation of seats in the Rajya Sabha to the states and Union Territories. At present the Rajya Sabha has 245 members.

(a) Representation of States :

- The seats are allotted to the states in the Rajya Sabha on the basis of population. Hence, the number of representatives varies from state to state. For example, Uttar Pradesh has 31 members while small states like Manipur, Mizoram and Tripura have one member each.

(b) Representation of Union Territories :

- The population of the Union Territories like Andaman-Nicobar, Chandigarh, Dadra & Nagar Haveli, Diu & Daman, Lakshadweep is too small to have any representative in the Rajya Sabha. Among the Union territories, Delhi, Jammu & Kashmir and Puducherry have 3, 4 and 1 representatives in the Rajya Sabha respectively. (As on Oct 2, 2019).

(c) Nominated Members :

- The President nominates 12 members to the Rajya Sabha from people who have special knowledge or practical experience in art, literature, science and social service. The rational behind this principle of nomination is to provide eminent persons a place in the Rajya Sabha without going through the process of election and the parliament and country should benefit from their expert knowledge and practical experience.

(d) Duration of the Rajya Sabha :

- The Rajya Sabha was first constituted in 1952 and is a continuing chamber, that is, it is a permanent body and not subject to dissolution. Article 83 of the Constitution deals with the duration of both the houses of the Parliament. However, one third of its members retire every second year. Their seats are filled up by fresh elections and presidential nominations at the beginning of every third year. The retiring members are eligible for re-election and renomination any number of times.
- The constitution has not fixed the term of office of members of the Rajya Sabha and left it to the parliament. Accordingly the parliament in the Representation of the People Act 1951, provided that the term of office of a member of the Rajya Sabha shall be 6 years.

Presiding Officers of Rajya Sabha :

(a) Chairman of Rajya Sabha :

- The presiding officer of the Rajya Sabha is known as the chairman. The Vice President of India is the ex-officio chairman of the Rajya Sabha. During any period when the vice president acts as the President or discharges the functions of the president, he does not perform the duties of the office of the chairman of Rajya Sabha.

(b) Deputy Chairman of Rajya Sabha :

- The Deputy Chairman is elected by the Rajya Sabha itself from amongst its members. Whenever the office of the Deputy Chairman falls vacant, the Rajya Sabha elects another member to fill the vacancy.
- Salaries and allowances of the Chairman and Deputy Chairman of Rajya Sabha are determined by the parliament. They are charged on the consolidated fund of India.

(3) Lok Sabha :

Composition of Lok Sabha :

- Remember the members of the Lok Sabha are directly elected by the people of India. The 61st Constitutional Amendment Act changed the legal voting age from 21 years to 18 years.
- The maximum strength of the Lok Sabha is fixed at 552. Though the constitution has abandoned the system of communal

representation, it provides for the reservation of seats for Scheduled Castes and Scheduled Tribes in the Lok Sabha on the basis of population ratios.

- Article 81 of the Constitution deals with the composition of the Lok Sabha. It is as follows :

(a) Representation of states in Lok Sabha :

- The members of the Lok Sabha are directly elected from the territorial constituencies of the states and their strength should not exceed 530. The seats of the Lok Sabha are allotted to the states based on their population in accordance with the 1971 census. Uttar Pradesh has highest 80 seats while small states like Sikkim, Mizoram and Nagaland have 1 member each.

(b) Representation of Union Territories :

- The constitution has empowered the Parliament to prescribe the manner of choosing the representatives of the union territories in the Lok Sabha. Accordingly the Parliament has enacted the Union Territories direct election to the House of the People Act, 1965, by which the members of the Lok Sabha from the union territories are also chosen by direct election. The Delhi NCR has 7, Jammu and Kashmir has 5 and Ladakh, Andaman & Nicobar islands, Chandigarh, Dadra & Nagar Haveli, Daman & Diu, Lakshadweep and Puducherry have 1 Lok Sabha seat each. Total 19 seats are allotted to the Union territories.

(c) Nominated members :

- The president can nominate two members from the Anglo-Indian community if the community is not adequately represented in the Lok Sabha. Anglo Indian is a person residing in India whose father father's ancestors were of European origin and the person who is born to the parents residing in India and fulfilling the above conditions. Temporary residents aren't included in that. Originally, this provision was to operate till 1960, but has been extended till 2020 by the 95th Amendment Act, 2009.

Presiding officers of Lok Sabha :

- According to the Article 13, the speaker and deputy speaker are elected by the Lok Sabha from amongst its members as soon as may be after its first sitting. Whenever the office of the speaker or deputy speaker falls vacant, the Lok Sabha election another member to fill the vacancy.

1.1.2 Members of the Parliament-Qualification and Disqualification

Qualifications :

(1) The constitution lays down the following qualifications for the person to be elected a member of the Parliament according to the Article 84 :

(a) He must be a citizen of India.

(b) He must make and subscribe to an oath or affirmation before the person authorised by the Election Commission for this purpose. In his oath or affirmation, he swears

(c) To bear true faith and allegiance to the constitution of India; To uphold the Sovereignty and integrity of India.

(d) He must be not less than 30 years of age in the case of Rajya Sabha and not less than 25 years of age in the case of the Lok Sabha.

(d) He must possess other qualifications prescribed by the parliament.

(2) The Parliament has laid down the following additional qualifications in the Representation of Peoples Act 1951 :

(a) One must be registered as an elector for a parliamentary constituency. This is same in case of both the Rajya Sabha and Lok Sabha. The required candidate contesting an election to the Rajya Sabha from a particular state should be an elector in that particular state was dispensed with in 2003.

(b) He must be a member of a scheduled caste or scheduled tribe in any state or union territory, if he wants to contest a seat reserved for them. However, a member of Scheduled Caste or Scheduled Tribes can also contest a seat not reserved for them.

Disqualifications :

(1) Under the Article 102 of the Constitution, a person shall be disqualified for being elected as a member of parliament.

(a) If he holds any office of profit under the union or state government except that of a Minister or any other office exempted by parliament.

(b) If he is of unsound mind and stands so declared by a court.

(c) If he is an undischarged insolvent.

(d) If he is not a citizen of India or has voluntarily acquired the citizenship of a foreign state or is under any acknowledgement of allegiance to a foreign state.

(e) If he is so disqualified under any law made by parliament.

(2) The Parliament has laid down the following additional code as qualifications in the representation of People Act 1951 :

(a) He must not have been found guilty of certain election offences or corrupt practices in the elections.

(b) He must not have been convicted for any offences resulting in imprisonment for two or more years. But, the detention of a person under the preventive detention law is not a disqualification.

(c) He must not have failed to lodge an account of his election expenses within the time.

(d) He must not have any interest in government contracts, works or services.

(e) He must not be a director or managing agent or hold an office of profit in a corporation in which the government has at least 25% share.

(f) He must not have been dismissed from government service for corruption or disloyalty to the state.

(g) He must have been convicted for promoting enmity between different groups or offence of bribery.

(h) He must not have been punished for preaching and practicing social crimes such as Untouchability, Dowry and Sati.

- On the question whether a member is subject to any of the above disqualifications, the president's decision is final. However, he should obtain the opinion of the Election Commission and act accordingly (Article 103).

(3) Disqualification on ground of defection :

- The constitution also lays down that a person shall be disqualified from being a member of parliament if he is so disqualified on the ground of defection under the provisions of the tenth schedule, article 102(2) and 191(2). A member incurs disqualification under the defection law:

(a) If he voluntarily gives up the membership of the political party on whose ticket he is elected to the house;

(b) If he votes or abstains from voting in the house contrary to any direction given by his political party;

(c) If any independently elected member joins any political party;

(d) If any nominated member joins any political party after the expiry of 6 months.

- The question of disqualification under the tenth schedule is decided by the chairman in case of Rajya Sabha and speaker in the case of Lok Sabha. In 1992, the Supreme Court ruled that the decision of the chairman or speaker in this regard is subject to Judicial review.

Vacating Seats in the Parliament :

(1) A person cannot be a member of both houses of Parliament at the same time.

Thus, the Representation of People Act 1951 provides for the following :

(a) If a person is elected to both the houses of Parliament, he must intimate within 10 days in which house he desires to serve. In default of such intimation, his seat in the Rajya Sabha becomes vacant.

(b) If a sitting member of one house is also elected to the other house, his seat in the first house becomes vacant.

(c) If a person is elected to two seats in a house he should exercise his option in for one. Otherwise, both sides become vacant.

(d) Similarly, a person cannot be a member of both the Parliament and state legislature at the same time. If a person is so elected, his seat in Parliament becomes vacant if he does not resign his seat in the state legislature within 14 days.

(2) Disqualification :

- If a member of parliament becomes subject to any of the disqualifications specified in the constitution, his seat becomes vacant. Here, the list of disqualifications also include the disqualification on the grounds of defection under the provisions of the tenth schedule of the constitution.

(3) Resignation :

- A member may resign his seat by writing to the chairman of Rajya Sabha or speaker of Lok Sabha, as the case may be. The seat Falls vacant when the resignation is accepted. However, the Chairman/ Speaker may not accept the resignation if he is satisfied that it is not voluntary or genuine.

(4) Absence :

- A House can declare the seat of a member vacant if he is absent from all its meetings for a period of 60 days without its permission. In computing the period of 60 days, no account shall be taken of any period during which the house is prorogued or adjourned for more than four consecutive days.

(5) Other cases :

- A member has to vacate his seat in the parliament :
  (a) If his election is declared void by the court;
  (b) If he is expelled by the house;
  (c) If he is elected to the office of president or vice president;
  (d) If he is appointed to the office of governor of a state.

1.1.3 Power and Functions of the Parliament:

Fundamental Powers and Functions :

- Constitutional expert Subhash Kashyap in his book 'Hamari Sansad' noted in it's chapter 3 'Sansad ke Kaam' that the functions of today's Parliament are not just making laws and regulations; at present this institution performs various roles which are interrelated hence hard to distinguish. Some people emphasize only on one or two aspects of it. Describing and determining completely the role of the parliament in the present scenario of modern parliamentary political science can be confusing. Still to get our thoughts clear about it; we can describe some basic functions and roles of the Parliament-
  (1) Political and Financial control;
  (2) Superintendence on administration;
  (3) Power to seek information;
  (4) Representation, to complain, to punish or to warn;
  (5) To resolve disputes and uphold National unity;

- According to Dr. Subhash Kashyap and M. Laxmikant in the Indian politico-administrative system, the Parliament occupies a central position and has a multifunctional role. It enjoys extensive powers and performs overactive functions towards the fulfillment of its constitutionally expected role. Those powers are as follows-

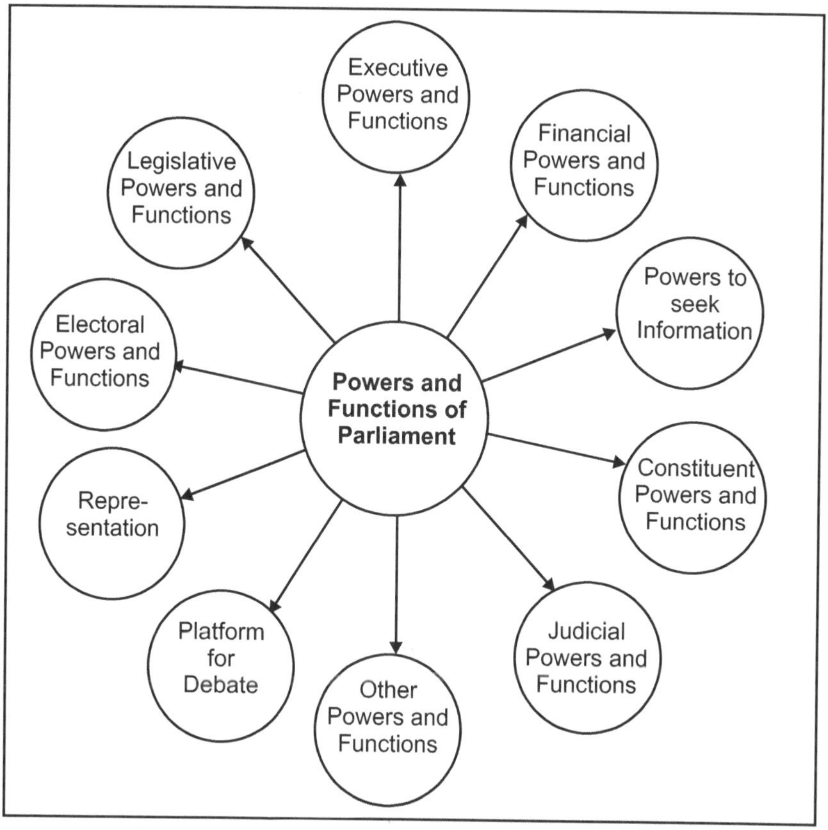

Fig. 1.1 : Powers and Functions of Parliament

(1) Legislative Powers and Functions :

- The Parliament of India can make laws for any part of the country. Though it's the highest legislative body; it only approves the bills prepared by the bureaucracy on the direction of the executive. The purpose and time to present the bill in the parliament is decided by the executive. Any important bill isn't presented in the parliament without the approval of the executive. Other members of the Parliament can introduce private bills in the parliament, but their approval without the support of the government is very unlikely.

- The primary function of the Parliament is to make laws for the Governance of a country. It has exclusive powers to make laws on the subjects enumerated in the union list which currently has 98 subjects. Originally, there were 97 which were increased to 100. (101st Constitutional Amendment Act 2016 reduced it to 98). And on the Residue subjects that is subject not enumerated in any of the three lists. With regard to the Concurrent list which has at present 52 subjects, originally had 47 subjects. The Parliament has overriding powers, that is the law of the Parliament prevails over the law of the state legislature in case of a conflict between the two.
- The constitution also empowers the Parliament to make laws on the subjects enumerated in the state list which at present has 61 subjects, originally 66 subjects, under the following five abnormal circumstances:

(a) When Rajya Sabha passes a resolution to that effect.

(b) When a proclamation of National Emergency is in operation.

(c) When two or more states make a joint request to the parliament.

(d) When necessary to give effect to International agreements, treaties and conventions.

(e) When president's rule is in operation in the state.

- The president can issue ordinances when the parliament is not in session. All the ordinances issued by the president during the Recess of the Parliament must be approved by the Parliament within 6 weeks after its reassembly. An ordinance becomes inoperative if it is not approved by the Parliament within that period.
- The Parliament makes laws in a skeleton for an unauthorised executive to make detailed rules and regulations within the framework of the parent law. This is known as delegated legislation or executive legislation or subordinate legislation. Such rules and regulations are placed before the Parliament for its examination.

(2) Executive Powers and Functions :

- The Constitution of India established a parliamentary form of Government in which the executive is responsible to the parliament for its policies and acts. Hence, the parliament exercises control over the executive through question hour, zero hour, half an hour discussion, short duration discussion calling attention motion, adjournment motion no confidence motion, censure motion.
- The executive continues in the office so long as he enjoys the confidence of the majority members in the Lok Sabha. In other words, the Council of Ministers can be removed from office by the Lok Sabha by passing a no confidence motion. The Lok Sabha can also express lack of confidence in the government.

(3) Financial Powers and Functions :

- No tax can be levied or collected and no expenditure can be encouraged by the executive except under the authority and with the approval of the parliament. Hence, the budget is placed before the Parliament for its approval. Enactment of the budget by the Parliament legalizes the receipts and expenditure of the government for the ensuing financial year.
- The Parliament also scrutinizes government spending and financial performance in order to avoid the illegal, irregular, unauthorized, improper usage and wastage and extravagance in public expenditure.

(4) Power to Seek Information :

- Power to seek information is one of the most important privileges the parliament has in order to discharge its duties and functions. The parliament has unrestrained powers to seek information. Only in exceptional cases like information affecting the national security or national integrity the executive is supposed to provide all the necessary information to the parliament via ministers. This information is considered important and it can be published in order to use it for discussion or debates and raising questions. Members can get information by raising questions to the executive in the parliament. Members can point out the mistakes or irregularities of the executive through these questions.

(5) Constituent Powers and Functions :

- The parliament is vested with the power to amend the constitution under Article 368 of the constitution by way of addition, variation or repeal of any provision. The major part of the Constitution can be amended by the parliament with special majority, that is, a majority (that is more than 50%) of the total membership of each house and a majority of not less than two thirds of the members present and voting in each house. Some other provisions of the Constitution can be amended by the Parliament with simple majority, that is, a majority of the members present and voting in each house of the parliament.
- Only a few provisions of the Constitution can be amended by the Parliament (by special majority) and with the consent of at least half of the state legislatures (simple majority). However, the power to initiate the process of the amendment of the Constitution in all the three cases lies exclusively in the hands of the parliament and not the state legislature.

(6) Judicial Powers and Functions :

- Judicial powers and functions of the Parliament are as follows : The Parliament can impeach the president for the violation of the constitution. It can remove the Vice President from his office. It can recommend the removal of judges including the Chief Justice of the Supreme Court and High Courts, Chief Election Commissioner, Comptroller and Auditor General of India to the president. The Parliament can punish its members or outsiders for the breach of its privileges or its contempt.

(7) Electoral Powers and Functions :

- The parliament participates in the election of the president along with the state legislative assemblies and elects the Vice President.

The Lok Sabha elects the speaker and deputy speaker, while the Rajya Sabha elects its Deputy Chairman.

- The parliament is also authorised to make laws to regulate the elections to the offices of President and Vice President, to both the houses of Parliament and to both the houses of state legislatures. Accordingly, parliament enacted the Presidential and Vice Presidential Election Act 1952, the Representation of People Act 1950, the Representation of People Act 1951 etc. cetera.

(8) Representation :

- The parliament represents different regions, social groups, economic or religious groups and communities and diverse cultures and ideologies.

(9) Platform for the Debate :

- The parliament is the highest platform of debates and discussion. Its power to exchange thoughts, ideas and debates is unrestrained. Members of the parliament have freedom of speech in the house. In this way, the parliament scrutinizes every subject of the country. Debates, discussions, ascent, dissent and inclusiveness is the soul of the democracy.

(10) Other Powers and functions :

(a) It serves as the highest deliberative body in the country. It discusses various issues of national and international significance.

(b) It approves all the three types of emergencies that is national, state and financial emergency proclaimed by the president.

(c) It can create or abolish the state legislative councils on the recommendation of the concerned state legislative assemblies.

(d) It can increase or decrease the area, alter the boundaries and change the names of states of the Indian Union.

(e) It can regulate the organisation and jurisdiction of the Supreme court and high courts and can establish a common High Court for two or more States.

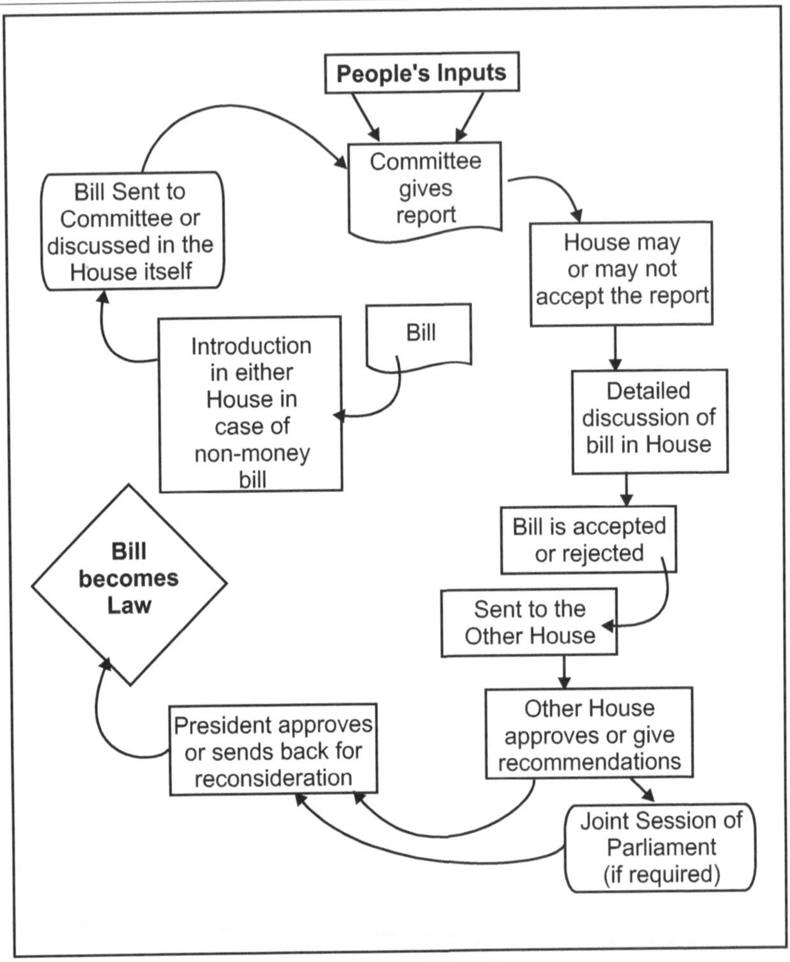

Fig. 1.2 : Law Making Process

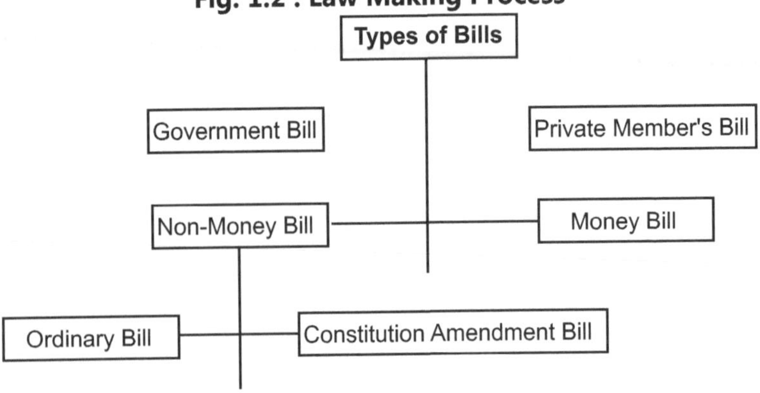

Fig. 1.3 : Types of Bills

Table No. 1.1 : Important Articles of the parliament

Article No.	Subject-Matter
79	Constitution of Parliament
80	Composition of the Council of States
81	Composition of the House of the People
82	Readjustment after each census
83	Duration of Houses of Parliament
84	Qualification for membership of Parliament
85	Sessions of Parliament, prorogation and dissolution
86	Right of President to address and send messages to Houses
87	Special address by the President
88	Rights of Ministers and Attorney-General as respects Houses
Officer of Parliament	
89	The Chairman and Deputy Chairman of the Council of States
90	Vacation and resignation of, and removal from, the office of Deputy Chairman
91	Power of the Deputy Chairman or other person to perform the duties of the office of, or to act as, Chairman
92	The Chairman or the Deputy Chairman not to preside while a resolution for his removal from office is under consideration
93	The Speaker and Deputy Speaker of the House of the People
94	Vacation and resignation of, and removal from, the offices of Speaker and Deputy Speaker
95	Power of the Deputy Speaker or other person to perform the duties of the office of, or to act as, Speaker
96	The Speaker or the Deputy Speaker not to preside while a resolution for his removal from office is under consideration

97	Salaries and allowances of the Chairman and Deputy Chairman and the Speaker and Deputy Speaker
98	Secretariat of Parliament
Conduct of Business	
99	Oath or affirmation by members
100	Voting in Houses, power of Houses to act notwithstanding vacancies and quorum
Disqualifications of Members	
101	Vacation of seats
102	Disqualifications for membership
103	Decision on questions as to disqualifications of members
104	Penalty for sitting and voting before making oath or affirmation under article 99 or when not qualified or when disqualified
Powers, Privileges and Immunities of Parliament and its Members	
105	Powers, privileges, etc., of the Houses of Parliament and of the members and committees thereof
106	Salaries and allowances of members
Legislative Procedure	
107	Provisions as to introduction and passing of Bills
108	Joint sitting of both Houses in certain cases
109	Special procedure in respect of Money Bills
110	Definition of "Money Bills"
111	Assent to Bills
Procedures in Financial Matters	
112	Annual financial statement
113	Procedure in Parliament with respect to estimates
114	Appropriation Bills
115	Supplementary, additional or excess grants
116	Votes on account, votes of credit and exceptional grants
117	Special provisions as to financial Bills

Procedure Generally	
118	Rules of procedure
119	Regulation by law of procedure in Parliament in relation to financial business
120	Language to be used in Parliament
121	Restriction on discussion in Parliament
122	Courts not to inquire into proceedings of Parliament
Legislative Powers of the President	
123	Power of President to promulgate Ordinances during recess of Parliament

Map of India After 31 October,2019

Table 1.2 : Statewise Distribution of Members of Parliament

Sr. No.	States/Union Territories	Rajya Sabha Members	Lok Sabha Member
1.	Andhra Pradesh	11	25
2.	Arunachal Pradesh	1	2
3.	Assam	7	14
4.	Bihar	16	40
5.	Chattisgarh	5	11
6.	Goa	1	2
7.	Gujarat	11	26
8.	Haryana	5	10
9.	Himachal Pradesh	3	4
10.	Jharkhand	6	14
11.	Karnataka	12	28
12.	Kerala	9	20
13.	Madhya Pradesh	11	29
14.	Maharashtra	19	48
15.	Manipur	1	2
16.	Meghalaya	1	2
17.	Mizoram	1	1
18.	Nagaland	1	1
19.	Odisha	10	21
20.	Punjab	7	13
21.	Rajasthan	10	25
22.	Sikkim	1	1
23.	Tamil Nadu	18	39
24.	Tripura	1	2
25.	Uttarakhand	3	5
26.	Uttar Pradesh	31	80
27.	West Bengal	16	42
28.	Telangana	07	17

Table No. 1.3 : Union Territories of India

Sr. No.	Union Territories	Members of Rajya Sabha	Members of Lok Sabha
1.	Andaman and Nicobar Islands	-	1
2.	Chandigarh	-	1
3.	Dadra and Nagar Haveli	-	1
4.	Daman and Diu	-	1
5.	Ladakh	-	1
6.	Jammu and Kashmir	4	5
7.	Lakshadweep	3	7
8.	Puducherry (Pondicherry)	-	1
9.	Ladakh	1	1
	Nominated Members	**12**	**2**

1.2 State Legislature : Structure, Power and Role

1.2.1 Composition of the State Legislature

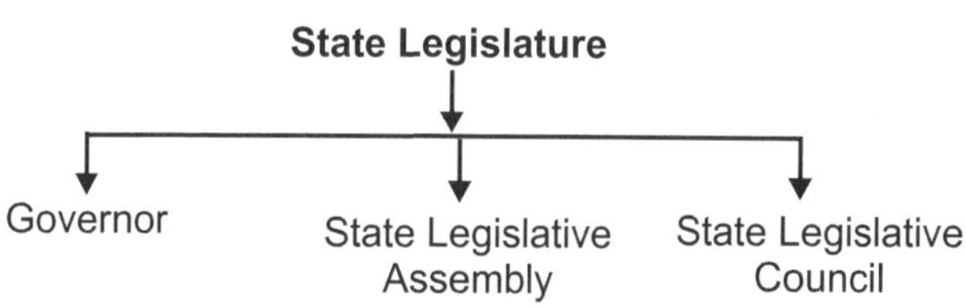

Fig. 1.4 : State Legislature

- The State Legislature occupies a pre-eminent and central position in the political system of a state. Article 168 to 212 in part 6 of the constitution deals with the organization, composition, duration, officers, procedures, privileges, powers and so on of the state Legislature.

1.2.2 Power and Functions of the State Legislature

The State Legislature is composed of the Governor, state legislative assembly and state legislative council.

(1) Governor : Article 153 of the constitution provides for a Governor to every state. Sometimes the same person can be appointed as a Governor for two or more states. The tenure of the governor is 5 years according to the Article 156 of the constitution but he remains in the office at the pleasure of the president. It can't be challenged according to Article 156 therefore there's no guaranteed or fixed tenure for the office of the Governor; the President can remove him from the office at any time. (Surya Narayan vs Union of India). The constitution lays down that the person who is to be appointed as governor should be a citizen of India and he should have completed the age of 35 years. He should not be a member of either House of the Parliament or house of the state legislature. If any such person is appointed as governor, he is deemed to have vacated his seat in that house on the date on which he enters upon his office as the Governor. We will study the powers, functions and role of the Governor in the topic executive.

(2) State Legislative Assembly :

Organization of the State Legislative Assembly :

(a) Strength of the members and their election

(b) Nominated members

(c) Duration of the Assembly

(d) Presiding Officers of the State Legislature

(a) Strength of the Members and their Election :

- The Legislative Assembly consists of representatives that are directly elected by the people on the basis of Universal adult franchise. Its maximum strength is fixed at 500 and minimum strength at 60. It means that its strength varies from 60 to 500 depending on the population size of the state. However, in case of Arunachal Pradesh, Sikkim and Goa, the minimum number is fixed at 30 and in case of Mizoram and Nagaland it is 40 and 46 respectively.

- For the purpose of holding direct elections to the Assembly, each state is divided into territorial constituencies. The demarcation of these constituencies is done in such a manner that the ratio between the population of each constituency and the number of seats allotted to it is the same throughout the state. The constitution provided for the reservation of seats for Scheduled Castes and Scheduled Tribes in the Assembly of each state on the basis of population ratios. Originally, this reservation was to operate for 10 years that is up to 1960. But this duration has been extended continuously since then by 10 years each time. Now, under the 95th Amendment Act of 2009, this reservation is to last until 2020.

(b) Nominated Members :

- The Governor can nominate one member from the Anglo Indian Community, if the community is not adequately represented in the Assembly. Anglo Indian person means a person residing in India whose father or ancestors were of European origin or a person who was born to the parents living in India. It does not include the people who are living in India temporarily. Originally, this provision was to operate for 10 years that is up to 1960. But this duration has been extended continuously since then by 10 years each time. Now, under the 95th Amendment Act of 2009, this is to last until 2020.

(c) Duration of the Assembly :

Like the Lok Sabha, the Legislative Assembly is not a continuing chamber. Its normal term is five years from the date of its first meeting after the general elections. the expiration of the period of 5 years operates as automatic dissolution of the assembly. However, the Governor is authorised to dissolve the Assembly at any time that is given before the completion of 5 years.

- The term of the assembly can be extended during the period of National Emergency by a law of Parliament for one year at a time for any length of time. However, this extension cannot continue beyond a period of six months after the emergency has ceased to operate. This means that the Assembly should be re-elected within 6 months after the revocation of emergency.

(d) Presiding Officers of the Assembly :

- Each house of the state legislature has its own presiding officer. There is a speaker and deputy speaker for the Legislative Assembly.
- **Speaker of Assembly :** The speaker is elected by the Assembly itself from amongst its members. Usually, the speaker remains in office during the life of the assembly. However, he vacates his office either in any of the three cases- if he ceases to be a member of the assembly; or if he resigns by writing to the deputy speaker; and if he is removed by a resolution passed by a majority of all the then members of the assembly. Such a resolution can be moved only after giving 14 days advance notice.

Powers and Functions of the Speaker :

(1) He maintains order and decorum in the Assembly for conducting its business and regulating its proceedings. This is his primary responsibility and he has the final power in this regard.

(2) The speaker is the final interpreter of the provisions of the Constitution of India, the rules of procedure and conduct of business of assembly and legislative precedents within the Assembly.

(c) He adjourns the Assembly or suspends the meeting in the absence of a quorum.

(d) He does not vote in the first instance but he can exercise a casting vote in the case of a tie.

(e) He decides whether the bill is a, Money Bill or not and his decision on this question is final.

(f) He appoints the chairmen of all committees of the assembly and supervises their functioning. He himself is the chairman of the business advisory committee, the rules committee and the general purpose committee.

(g) He decides the questions of disqualification of a member of the assembly, arising on the ground of defection under the provisions of the tenth schedule.

(h) He can allow a 'secret' sitting of the house at the request of the leader of the house.

Deputy Speaker of Assembly :

- Like the speaker, the deputy speaker is also elected by the Assembly itself from amongst its members. He is elected after the election of the speaker has taken place. Like the speaker, the deputy speaker remains in office usually during the life of the assembly. However, he also vacates his office earlier if he ceases to be a member of the Assembly; or if he resigns by writing to the speaker; and if he is removed by a resolution passed by a majority of all the then members of the assembly. Such a resolution can be moved only after giving 14 days advance notice.
- The deputy speaker performs the duties of the speaker's office when it is vacant. He also acts as the speaker when the latter is absent from a sitting of the assembly. In both cases, he has all the powers of the speaker. The speaker nominates from amongst the members a panel of chairmen. Any one of them can preside over the assembly in the absence of the speaker or the deputy speaker. He has the same powers as the speaker when so presiding. He holds office until the new panel of chairmen is nominated.

1.2.3 State Legislative Council

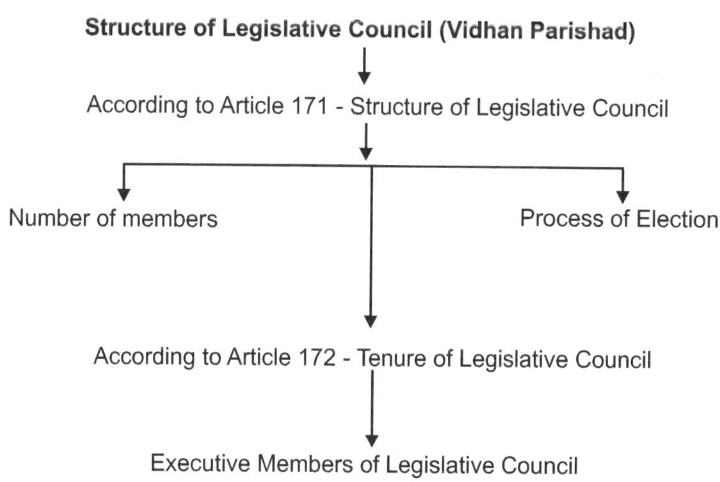

Fig. 1.5 : Structure of Legislative Assembly

Composition of Council :

(1) Strength : Unlike the members of the Legislative Assembly, the members of the legislative council are indirectly elected. The maximum strength of the Council is fixed at one third of the total strength of the assembly and the minimum strength is fixed at 40. It means that the size of the Council depends on the size of the assembly of the concerned state. This is done to ensure the predominance of a directly elected house in the legislative affairs of the state.

(2) Manner of Election : Of the total number of members of the Legislative Council :

(a) One third are elected by the members of local bodies in the state like municipalities, district boards etc.

(b) $1/12^{th}$ are elected by graduates of 3 years Standing and residing within the state.

(c) 1/12 are elected by teachers of 3 years standing in the state, not lower in standard than Secondary School.

(d) One third are elected by the members of the Legislative Assembly of the state from amongst persons who are not members of the assembly.

(e) The remaining one sixth are nominated by the Governor from amongst persons who have special knowledge or practical experience of literature, science, arts, cooperative movement and social service.

- Thus, $5/6^{th}$ of the total number of members of the Legislative Council are indirectly elected and $1/6^{th}$ are nominated by the Governor. The members are elected in accordance with the system of proportional representation by means of Single Transferable Vote. The bonafides or propriety of the governor's nomination in any case cannot be challenged in the courts.
- This scheme of composition of the Legislative Council as laid down in the constitution is tentative and not final. The parliament is authorised to modify or replace the same. However, it has not enacted any such law so far.

(3) Duration of Council : Like the Rajya Sabha, the Legislative Council is a continuing chamber, that is, it is a permanent body and is not subject to dissolution. But, one third of its members retire on the expiration of every second year. So, a member continues as such for 6 years. The vacant seats are filled up by elections and nominations by the Governor at the beginning of every third year. The retiring members are also eligible for re-election and renomination any number of times.

(4) Presiding Officers of the Council :

(a) Chairman of Council : The chairman is elected by the Council itself from amongst its members. The chairman vacates his office if, he ceases to be a member of the Council, or if he resigns by writing to the Deputy Chairman; and if he is removed by a resolution passed by a majority of all the then members of the Council. Such a resolution can be moved only after giving 14 days advance notice.

- As a presiding officer, the powers and functions of the chairman in the Council are similar to those of the speaker in the Assembly. However, the speaker has one special power which is not enjoyed by the chairman. The speaker of the Assembly decides whether the bill is a money bill or not and his decision on this question is final.

(b) Deputy Chairman of Council : Like the chairman, the Deputy Chairman is also elected by the Council itself from amongst its members. The Deputy Chairman vacates his office if, he ceases to be a member of the Council, or if he resigns by writing to the chairman; and if he is removed by a resolution passed by a majority of all the then members of the Council. Such a resolution can be moved only after giving 14 days advance notice.

- The Deputy Chairman performs the duties of the chairman's office when it is vacant. He also acts as the chairman when the latter is absent from the sitting of the Council. In both the cases, he has all the powers of the chairman. The chairman nominates from amongst the members a panel of vice chairmen. Any one of them can preside over the council in the absence of the chairman or the Deputy Chairman. He has the same powers as the chairman when so presiding. He holds office until a new panel of vice chairman is nominated.

Membership of State Legislature :

Qualification (in constitution) :

(1) He must be a citizen of India.

(2) He must make and subscribe to an oath or affirmation before the person authorised by the election commission for this purpose. In his oath or affirmation, he swears.

- To bear true faith and allegiance to the constitution of India.
- To uphold the sovereignty and integrity of India.

(3) He must be not less than 30 years of age in the case of the Legislative Council and not less than 25 years of age in the case of Legislative Assembly.

(4) He must possess other qualifications prescribed by the parliament.

Qualifications according to the Representation of People Act 1951 :

(1) A person to be elected to the Legislative Council must be an elector for an Assembly Constituency in the concerned state and to be qualified for the Governor nomination, he must be a resident in the concerned state.

(2) A person to be elected to the Legislative Assembly must be an elector for an Assembly Constituency in the concerned state.

(3) He must be a member of scheduled caste or scheduled tribe if he wants to contest a seat reserved for them. However, a member of scheduled caste or scheduled tribe can also contest a seat not reserved for them.

Disqualification (Laid down by the Constitution) :

(1) If the person holds any office of profit under the union or state government except that of a Minister or any other office exempted by State legislature.

(2) If he is of unsound mind and stands so declared by a court.

(3) If he is an undischarged insolvent.

(4) If he is not a citizen of India or has voluntarily acquired a citizenship of foreign state or is under any acknowledgement of allegiance to a foreign state.

(5) If he is so disqualified under any law made by parliament.

Disqualifications under Representation of People Act, 1951

(1) He must not have been found guilty or any corrupt practices in the elections.

(2) He must not have been convicted for any offence resulting in imprisonment for two or more years. But, the detention of a person under a preventive detention law is not a disqualification.

(3) He must not have failed to lodge an account of his election expenses within the time.

(4) He must not have any interest in government contracts, works or services.

(5) He must not be a director or managing agent nor hold an office of profit in a corporation in which government has at least 25% share.

(6) He must have been dismissed from government service for corruption or disloyalty to the state.

(7) He must not have been convicted for promoting enmity between different groups or for the offence of bribery.

(8) He must not have been punished for preaching and practicing social crimes such as Untouchability, Dowry and Sati.

- On the question whether a member has become subject to any of the above disqualifications, the governors decision is final. However, he should obtain the opinion of the election commission and act accordingly.

Disqualification on ground of defection : The constitution also lays down that a person shall be disqualified for being a member of either House of state legislature if he is so disqualified on the ground of defection under the provisions of the tenth schedule. The question of disqualification under the tenth schedule is decided by the chairman, in the case of Legislative Council and, speaker, in the case of Legislative Assembly.

Powers and Functions of the State Legislature :

(1) Collective Privileges :

(a) It has the right to publish its reports, debates and proceedings and also the right to prohibit others from publishing the same.

(b) It can exclude strangers from its proceedings and hold secret sittings to discuss some important matters.

(c) It can make rules to regulate its own procedure and conduct its business and to adjudicate upon such matters.

(d) It can punish members as well as outsiders for breach of its privileges its contempt by reprimand admonition or imprisonment. Also suspension or expulsion in case of members.

(e) It can institute enquiries and order the attendance of witnesses and send for relevant papers and records.

(f) It has the right to receive immediate information of the arrest and detention, conviction, imprisonment and release of a member.

(g) The courts are prohibited to inquire into the proceedings of a house or its committees.

(h) No person either a member or outsider can be arrested, and no legal process civil or criminal can be served within the precincts of the house without the permission of the presiding officer.

(2) Individual Privileges :

(a) A member cannot be arrested during the session of the state legislature and 40 days before the beginning and 40 days after the end of such session. This privilege is available only in civil cases and not in criminal cases for preventive detention cases.

(b) They have freedom of speech in the state legislature. No member is liable to any proceeding in any Court for anything said or any vote given by him in the state legislature for its committees. This freedom is subject to the provisions of the constitution and to rules and standing orders regulating the procedure of the state legislature.

(c) They are exempted from jury service. They can refuse to give evidence and appear as a witness in a case pending in court when the state legislature is in session.

Legislative procedure in state legislature :

(1) Ordinary Bills :

(a) Bill in the originating house
(b) Bill in the second house
(c) Assent of the governor
(d) Assent of the president

(2) Money Bill : Money bill cannot be introduced in the Legislative Council. It can be introduced in the Legislative Assembly only and that too on the recommendation of the Governor. Every such bill is considered to be a government bill and can be introduced only by a Minister. After a money bill is passed by the legislative Assembly, it is transmitted to the legislative council for its consideration. The Legislative Council cannot reject or amend a Money bill. It can only make recommendations and must return the bill to the Legislative Assembly within 14 days. If the Legislative Council does not return the bill to the Legislative Assembly within 14 days, the bill is deemed to have been passed by both the houses.

Table No. 1.4 : State Legislature in General

Article	General
153.	Governors of State.
154.	Executive Power of State.
155.	Appointment of Governor .
156.	Term of office of Governor.
157.	Qualifications for Appointment as Governor.
158.	Conditions of Governor's office.
159.	Oath or affirmation by the Governor.
160.	Discharge of the functions of the Governor in certain contingencies.
161.	Power of Governor to grant pardons, etc., and to suspend, remit 161 or commute sentences in certain cases.
162.	Extent of executive power of State. Council of Ministers.

Council of Ministers

163.	Council of Ministers to aid and advise Governor.
164.	Other provisions as to ministers. The Advocate-General for the State.

The Advocate - General for the State

165.	Advocate-General for the State.
166.	Conduct of Business of the Government of a State.

Conduct of Government Business

167.	Duties of Chief Minister as respects furnishing of information to Governor, etc.

General

168.	Constitution of Legislatures in States.
169.	Abolition or creation of Legislative Councils in States.
170.	Composition of the Legislative Assemblies.
171.	Composition of the Legislative Councils.
172.	Duration of State Legislatures.
173.	Qualification for membership of the State Legislature.
174.	Sessions of the State Legislature prorogation and dissolution.
175.	Right of Governor to address and send messages to the House or Houses.
176.	Special address by the Governor.
177.	Rights of Ministers and Advocate-General as respects the Houses.

Officers of the State Legislature

178.	The speaker and Deputy Speaker of the Legislative Assembly.
179.	Vacation and resignation of and removal from the offices of Speaker and Deputy Speaker.
180.	Power of the Deputy Speaker or other person to perform the duties of the office of or to act as, Speaker.

181.	The Speaker or the Deputy Speaker not to preside while a resolution for his removal from office is under consideration.
182.	The Chairman and Deputy Chairman of the Legislative Council.
183.	Vacation and resignation of, and removal from, the offices of Chairman and Deputy Chairman.
184.	Power of the Deputy Chairman or other person to perform the duties of the office of, or to act as, Chairman.
185.	The Chairman or the Deputy Chairman not to preside while a resolution for his removal from office is under consideration.
186.	Salaries and allowances of the Speaker and Deputy Speaker and the Chairman and Deputy Chairman.
187.	Secretariat of State Legislature.

Conduct of Business

188.	Oath or affirmation by members.
189.	Voting in Houses, power of Houses to act notwithstanding vacancies and quorum.

Disqualifications of Members

190.	Vacation of seats.
191.	Disqualifications for membership.
192.	Decision on question as to disqualifications of members.
193.	Penalty for sitting and voting before maing oath or affirmation under article 188 or when not qualified or when disqualified.
194.	Powers, privileges, etc., of the Houses of Legislatures and of the members and committees thereof.
195.	Salaries and allowances of members.

Legislative Procedure

196.	Provisions as to introduction and passing of Bills.
197.	Restriction on powers of Legislative Council as to Bills other than Money Bills.

198.	Special procedure in respect of Money Bills.
199.	Definition of "Money Bills".
200.	Assent to Bills.
201.	Bills reserved for consideration.

Procedure in Financial Matters

202.	Annual financial Statement.
203.	Procedure in Legislature with respect to estimates.
204.	Appropriation Bills.
205.	Supplementary, additional or excess grants.
206.	Votes on account, votes of credit and exceptional grants.
207.	Special provisions as to financial Bills.

Procedure Generally

208.	Rules of procedure.
209.	Regulation by law procedure in the Legislature of the State in relation to
210.	Language to be used in the Legislature.
211.	Restriction on discussion in the Legislature.
212.	Courts not to inquire into proceedings of the Legislature.

✧ QUESTIONS ✧

Q. I : Answer the following questions in short :

(1) *From which language the name of State Legislature and Union Legislature have been taken ?*

(2) *Under which article of the Constitution the parliament of India consists of ?*

(3) *Who are the member of the Indian Legislature ?*

(4) *The president nominates. How many members of the Rajya Sabha ?*

(5) *What is the maximum strength of Rajya Sabha members ? Who are they ?*

(6) *What is the maximum strength of the Lok Sabha ?*

(7) *What is meant by Anglo Indian members ?*

(8) *Name the States and Union Territories of India.*

(9) *State the composition of State Legislature.*

(10) *State the composition of Legislative Council ?*

(11) *State the Representation of Union Territories of the Indian Legislature.*

(12) *What is the minimum age criteria to become a member of Lok Sabha and Rajya Sabha.*

(13) *What are the qualifications for a person to be selected as a member of parliament ?*

(14) *Who appoints the Governor of a state ? What is the procedure?*

(15) *What is the maximum and minimum strength of the members of the State Legislative Assembly ?*

(16) *State the duration of State Legislative Assembly.*

(17) *What are some basic functions and role of the parliament ?*

Q. II : Write short notes on :

(1) *President*

(2) *Rajya Sabha*

(3) *Lok Sabha*

(4) *Union Legislature*

(5) *Presiding officers of Rajya Sabha*

(6) *State Legislative Assembly*

(7) *Speaker and Deputy Speaker of Legislative Assembly*

(8) *Speaker and Deputy speaker of Rajya Sabha*

(9) *Chairman and Deputy Chairman of State Legislative council*

(10) *Chairman and Deputy Chairman of the Council*

Q. III : Answer the following questions in 150 to 200 words :

(1) *State the composition of Lok Sabha.*

(2) *State the composition of Rajya Sabha.*

(3) *State the composition of Legislative Council.*

(4) *State the composition of House of States.*

(5) *State the structure of Indian Judiciary.*

(6) *Elaborate on the qualifications and disqualification of the members of the parliament.*

(7) *Elaborate on the qualifications and disqualification of the members of the state legislature.*

Q. IV : Answer the following questions in 500 words (in detail) :

(1) *Explain the powers and functions of the Parliament.*

(2) *Explain the powers and functions of the State Legislature.*

QUESTIONS FROM PREVIOUS EXAMINATIONS

Q. 1 : Answer the following questions in five to six sentences.

(1) Vidhan Sabha. **(April 2014)**

(2) Composition, functions and powers of Rajya Sabha. **(November 2014)**

(3) State the composition and powers of Union Legislature and State Legislature. **(Nov. 2014, April 2018)**

(4) State the powers and composition of Rajya Sabha. **(April 2015, Oct. 2015, Oct. 2018)**

(5) Speaker of Loksabha. **(Oct. 2015)**

(6) State the composition and powers of Lok Sabha. **(April 2016, April 2017, Oct. 2016)**

(7) State the composition and powers of Union Legislature. **(Oct 2017)**

(8) Speaker of Lok Sabha, write a short note. **(April 2018)**

❋ ❋ ❋

UNIT – 2

EXECUTIVE

SYNOPSIS

2.1 Union Executive

- Any administrative officer from an organisation has to take a decision and implement it. This process is called administration or management. But at the top of an organisation, there should be a group who can take a policy based decision and keep co-ordination among the members. In every organisation such types of groups are there. They work as a chief executive or Administrative officer in the Executive Department.
- The 1st branch of the government is called Administration which takes a policy based decision and which makes laws and regulations.
- The 2nd branch of the government implements these laws and regulations and is called as the Executive branch. The administrative branch participates in law making. The formal name of the administrative branch is different in different countries.

- Not only President, Prime minister and council of ministers are involved in the executive branch but all the administrative officers who are involved are responsible to all the government policies. But those who are involved in day to day responsibility constitute the permanent executive branch.
- In the Indian constitution part 5 Article 52 to 78 talks about the Executive Branch. In article 73 of the constitution internal expansion of power is done, on all these subjects only the parliament can take a decision. One thing to remember is that the use of executives is done according to the law of the constitution.
- President, Vice president, Prime Minister, Council of Ministers comptroller and Auditor General.

2.1.1 President :

- According to Article 52 of the constitution, the president of India is the Head of the country. He is the 1st citizen of the country and his priorities are Unity, Integrity and Prestige.

Selection : According to Article 55 of the Indian Constitution, the President is not directly elected by the people but he is elected by an electoral college in which Lok Sabha, Rajya Sabha and 2/3 of State Vidhan Sabha participate including members elected from the legislature of the union territories of Delhi, Pondichery, Jammu and Kashmir.

- The number of voting members in the electoral college who vote for the president is decided by the following formula :

  (1) Members elected from Vidhan Sabha Assembly is divided from the total population of the state.

  Values of Votes of Assembly Members

$$\frac{\text{State Population}}{\text{Electrol Members of State assembly}} \times \frac{1}{1000}$$

(2) Values of Parliamentary Members :

$$\frac{\text{Total values of all electoral member of Vidhan Sabha}}{\text{Total Numbers of both the houses of parliament}}$$

Tenure of President : According to article 56 of the Indian constitution, the day the president takes oath from that day to further 5 years. But the president and vice president can give their resignation before completing their duration willingly. According to article 61 if the president violates the constitution then there is a process of impeachment by which he can be removed from his post. Unless the next president is elected, the president enjoys the post.

Eligibility : Article 58 (1) citizen of India,

(2) Completed of 35 yrs. age.

(3) Eligible to be elected as Lok Sabha Member.

Conditions : (1) President will not be a member of State Legislature or parliament. If it is so, he will have to leave that post.

(2) He will not enjoy any profit post.

(3) President has authorized accommodation.

(4) Oath : Article 60 of the constitution. The chief justice of India gives oath to the president and if the chief justice is absent then any other judge of the Supreme court can give him oath.

(5) Process of Impeachment : Article 61- If the president exploits the constitution and if he is found guilty then the process of impeachment can be started by any of the houses. Atleast 1/4 of the members should sign and 14 days before a notice should be given to the president. Unless and until 2/3 majority accepts the guilt then only the impeachment process is done.

- According to Article 62 if the president resigns or expires then his vacant post is supposed to fill as early as possible. Till the new president is not elected, the vice president acts as the president.

Powers and Functions of the President :

(1) Executive Powers : All the work is done by his name Article 77.

(2) He appoints the Prime minister and council of Ministers.

(3) He appoints the Comptroller Auditor General Article 36. The CAG enjoys the post till the President's wish.

(4) He appoints Attorney General, Chief Election Commissioner and other Election officers, Chairman of Union Public Service Commission, Governor, and Chairmen of different commissions.

(5) He establishes the commission of SC, ST and other backward classes.

(6) He can ask the P.M. for the information of the Federal Administration.

(7) Prime Minster can ask the President to discuss on some issues if there has been no discussion between the P.M. and Council of Ministers.

(2) Legislative Powers :

(1) The President can call the session of both the houses of Parliament and he can also dissolve. He can dissolve the Lok Sabha. He can call a combined meeting or session of both the houses of Parliament.

(2) He addresses the 1st session after the new election of Lok Sabha.

(3) If both the Post of chairman and vice chairman is empty then he has the power to appoint the chairman and vice chairman.

(4) The President appoints 12 members for Rajya Sabha from the different fields and two Anglo Indian from Lok Sabha.

(5) The president forwards the report of C. A. G, UPSC Finance Commission to the parliament.

(6) If the parliament pass the amendment.

(7) The President can hold the amendment given by the state legislature. If the amendment is not an amendment then he can order to reform it again. He should give the permission is not necessary.

(8) In parts and list 3rd the president has legislative power during the released period.

(9) If there is no session in both the houses then the president can declare an order late the annual will be passed by both the houses within 6 weeks.

2.1.2 Vice President :

Article 63 says that there should be a Vice President for India.

Appointment : The Vice President is indirectly elected by members of an electoral college. The election process of the President and Vice President is the same.

Qualification :

(1) He should not be a member of any house and if so he has to resign from that post after becoming Vice President.
(2) Citizen of India.
(3) 35 years of age should be completed.
(4) He should not hold any office of profit.
(5) He must have qualifications to become the member of Rajya Sabha.

Tenure :

Article 67 5 years. (1) He can give his resignation letter to the President.

(2) The Vice President can be removed from his office after the resolution of the Rajya Sabha is agreed by the members of the Lok Sabha but for this he should be given a notice 14 days before.
(3) If his post is empty then within six months it should be filled.
(4) Article 69. The president or he has appointed any one member an give oath to the vice president.
(5) If the president is not his office for any reason then the vice president acts as a president till the new president is elected.

Rights and Functions :

He is a permanent President of Rajya Sabha. If the president is not in office for any reason then the vice president acts as a president till the new president is elected and he enjoys the power as a president of Rajya Sabha.

2.1.3 Prime Minister :

There is no process of appointment of the Prime Minister of India. Article 75 says President can appoint the Prime Minister from the Majority members of Lok Sabha.

Tenure : There is no proper duration of the Prime Minster, but he can hold his office till the President's wish. The Prime Minster takes the oath in the presence of the President.

Powers, Functions and Role :

(1) Leader of Lok Sabha : The Prime Minster often announces the major policy decisions of the government.

(2) **Leader of council of Ministers :** The Prime minister forms the ministry allots the departments and all the other members remain till the Prime Minister has a confidence. Many a time, the Prime Minster is a chair person for all the meetings, he is also the main leader of the parliament, main administrator.

(3) The Prime Minster is a key between the council of Ministers and the President.

Other Powers and Functions :

(1) He is a president of Niti Ayog, National development council, National Unity Council, International Council, water resources council.

(2) He plays an important role in making foreign, policies.

(3) He is an important speaker in the central government.

(4) Being the leader of the country, he visits different states to know their problems and issues.

(5) He is the leader of the ruling political party.

(6) He is the chief of all the services in the country.

Council of Ministers :

According article 74 there will be a Council of Ministers for the guidance of the president. According to 42nd amendment 1976 which made the advice binding on the president, 44th amendment 1979 has a slight change it empowers the president to return to the advice with or without changes.

Structure of the Council of Ministers : There is a 3 tier council of Ministers that is cabinet Ministers, State Ministers and Deputy Ministers.

(1) **Cabinet Ministers :** They are the head of the department. Mostly, this post goes to the senior members. The cabinet is the highest policy and decision making body. Normally, 15 to 20 members are there as cabinet Ministers.

(2) **Deputy Ministers :** They assist the cabinet Ministers. If department is very big then they get a change of a different section. Otherwise they help the cabinet ministers in day to day administration of the department.

(3) Deputy Ministers : These ministers are either attached to the cabinet ministers or the ministers of the state. They help their seniors in running the department, but they do not enjoy any independent decision making power.

(4) Parliamentary Secretary : They are the trainee ministers. They are appointed only to get the experience of running the ministry. They assist the Ministers in their parliament work.

2.2 State Executive

Part VI of the Indian Constitution deals with the States and their Executive Boards.

2.2.1 Governor :

Appointment Of Governor : The Governor of a State is appointed by the President. Article 153 says that there should be a Governor for each state. But under the 7th Amendment Act, 1956, the same person can be appointed as Governor of one or more States.

Term Of Office : He normally holds office for five years, but can be removed at any time before that by the President i.e. the Governor remains in office during the pleasure of the President. He may be asked to continue beyond the normal term of five years, until his successor enters upon his office. The Governor may resign at any time by writing to the President.

Qualifications : A person must be a citizen of India and must have completed the age of 35 years.

Conditions Of Office :

1. The Governor cannot be a member of Parliament or of a State Legislature and if a person is such a member at the time of the appointment as Governor, his seat in Parliament or the State Legislature, as the case may be, will become vacant on the date on which he assumes office as governor.
2. The Governor cannot hold any other office of profit during the term of his office.
3. He is entitled without payment of rent to the use of his official residence.

4. He is also entitled to such emoluments, allowances and privileges as may be determined by the Parliament.

Power And Functions Of Governor :

1. Executive powers
2. Legislative Powers
3. Financial Powers
4. Judicial Powers

(1) Executive powers

- All the executive functions in the State are carried on in the name of the Governor.
- He/she not only appoints the Chief Minister but on his/her advice appoints the members of the Council of Ministers.
- He/she appoints the Advocate- General and Chairman and members of the State Public Service Commission.
- A situation may arise when in the opinion of the Governor there is a breakdown of the constitutional machinery in the State. In such a case, the Governor may report the situation to the President for the imposition of President's Rule in that State. During such emergency, the Governor rules on behalf of the President.
- He acts as the chancellor of universities in the state. He also appoints the vice-chancellors of universities in the state.

(2) Legislative Powers

- It is in his power to prorogue the state legislature and dissolve the state legislative assemblies.
- He addresses the state legislature at the first session of every year.
- If the speaker of the legislative assembly is absent and so the Deputy Speaker, then the Governor appoints a person to preside over the session.
- Governor appoints ⅙ of the total members of the legislative council from the fields of Literature, Science, Art, Cooperative Movement, Social Service.
- He decides on the question of disqualification of members of the state legislature in consultation with the Election Commission.

- When a bill is sent to the governor after it is passed by the state legislature, he can give his assent to the bill or withhold his assent to the bill.
- He can promulgate ordinances when the state legislature is not in session. These ordinances must be approved by the state legislature within six weeks from its reassembly. He can also withdraw an ordinance at anytime. This is the most important legislative power of the governor
- He lays the reports of the State Finance Commission, the State Public Service Commission and the Comptroller and Auditor-General relating to the accounts of the state, before the state legislature.
- Return the bill (if it is not a money bill) for reconsideration of the state legislature . However, if the bill is passed again by the state legislature with or without amendments ,the governor has to give his assent to the bill.

(3) Financial Powers

- He looks over the state budget being laid in the state legislature.
- No money bill can be introduced in the State Legislative Assembly without the prior permission of the Governor.
- He recommends the demand for grants which otherwise, cannot be given.
- Contingency Fund of the State is under him and he makes appropriate provisions to meet an unforeseen expenditure.
- State Finance Commission is constituted every five years by him.

(4) Judicial Powers

- The Governor possesses the power to grant pardon reprieves, respites or remission of punishment or to suspend, remit or commute the sentence of any person convicted by the Courts of any offence against any law relating to a matter to which the executive power of the State extends.
- President consults the Governor while appointing judges of High Court
- In consultation with the state High Court, the Governor makes appointments, postings and promotions of the district judges.

- In consultation with the state high court and state public service commission, he also appoints persons to the judicial services.

Articles related to Governor

Articles	Provisions
153	Governors of states
155	Appointment of Governor
156	Term of office of Governor
157	Qualifications for appointment as Governor
158	Conditions of Governor's office
160	Discharge of the functions of the Governor in certain contingencies
161	Power of the Governor to grant pardons and others
175	Right of the Governor to address and send messages to the house or houses of the state legislature
176	Special address by the Governor
201	Bills reserved by the Governor for consideration of the President
213	Power of Governor to promulgate ordinances
217	Governor is consulted by the President in the matter of the appointments of the judges of the High Courts
233	Appointment of district judges by the Governor
234	Appointments of persons (other than district judges) to the judicial service of the state by the Governor

2.2.2 Chief Minister :

Appointment of Chief Minister :

- Indian constitution does not specifically mention about the qualification needed to be appointed as Chief Minister (CM).
- Article 164 of the Constitution envisages that the Chief Minister shall be appointed by the governor. However, this does not imply that the governor is free to appoint anyone as the Chief Minister of the state or UT.
- A leader of the party that has got the majority share of votes in the assembly elections, is appointed as the Chief Minister of the state. Chief Minister can belong to any house in the State Legislature.

Term of Chief Minister's office :

- The term of the Chief Minister is not fixed and he holds his office during the pleasure of the governor.
- Governor cannot remove him at any time. Governor cannot even dismiss him till the time he enjoys the support of the majority of the house.

Function and Power of the Chief Minister

1. In Relation to the Council of Ministers
2. In Relation to the State Legislature
3. In relation to Governor
4. Other Functions and powers

(1) In Relation to the Council of Ministers

- Chief Minister is the head of the Council of Ministers of his State.
- He recommends to the governor on who to appoint as ministers.
- He designates or reshuffles the portfolios of the ministers. He can ask a minister to resign or tell the governor to dismiss him.
- All activities of the ministers are guided and controlled by the Chief Minister.
- He coordinates the activities of all ministers. If he resigns, the entire council of ministers collapses.

(2) In Relation to the State Legislature

- He is the leader of the house. Before a governor prorogues and summons the sessions of the state legislature, the Chief Minister's advice is a must.
- Legislative Assembly can be dissolved at any time on his recommendation to the governor. All government policies are announced by him on the floor of the house.

(3) In relation to Governor

- According to Article 163, the governor is advised by the council of ministers which is headed by the Chief Minister.
- According to Article 164, the Governor appoints Chief Minister and later the Chief Minister recommends the Governor on the appointment of ministers and remains in office during the pleasure of the President.

- According to Article 167, the Chief Minister has to perform following duties :

(a) All the activities, decisions that are taken up by the council of ministers are communicated to the governor by the chief minister.

(b) To report to the governor, information about the administrative affairs if and when asked by the governor.

(c) If any minister has decided on any issue, the same has to be reported to the Governor by the Chief Minister when the same has not been considered by the council.

(d) He gives his advice to the governor for the appointment of the Advocate-General, Chairman of State Public Service commission, the state election commission, etc.

(4) Other Functions and powers :

- He chairs the State Planning Board.
- He is a member of Inter-State Council and National Development Council which are headed by the Prime Minister.
- He is the chief spokes person of the state government.
- As a leader of the state, he meets various sections of the people and receives memoranda from them regarding their problems and so on.

Important articles regarding chief minister -

- Article 163- The governor is advised by the council of ministers which is headed by the Chief Minister.
- Article 164 -Governor appoints the Chief Minister and later the Chief Minister recommends the Governor on the appointment of ministers.
- Article 166- conduct of business of Government of State.
- Article 167 - Chief Minister has to communicate all administrative decisions that are taken up by him and the council of ministers to the governor.

Sr. No.	Governor	from	to
1	Dr P. Subbarayan	17th April 1962	06th Oct. 1962
2	Vijaya Lakshmi Pandit	28th Nov. 1962	18th Oct. 1964
3	Dr P V Cherian	14th Nov. 64	08th Nov. 1969
4	Ali Yavar Jung	26th Feb. 70	11th Dec. 1976
5.	Sri Sadiq Ali	30th April 1977	3rd Nov. 1980
6	O P Mehra	03rd Nov. 1980	05th Mar. 1982
7	Idris Hasan Latif	06th Mar. 1982	16th April 1985
8	Kona Prabhakara Rao	31st May 1985	02th April 1986
9	Dr. Shankar Dayal Sharma	03rd April 1986	02th Sep. 1987
10	KasuBrahmananda Reddy	20th Feb. 1988	18th Jan. 1990
11	Dr. C Subramaniam	15th Feb.1990	09th Jan. 1993
12	Dr. P.C. Alexander	12th Jan. 1993	13th July 2002
13	Mohammed Fazal	10th Oct. 2002	05th Dec. 2004
14	S. M. Krishna	12th Dec. 2004	05th March 2008
15	S. C. Jamir	09th Mar. 2008	22nd Jan. 2010
16	Kateekal Sankaranarayanan	22nd Jan. 2010	24th Aug. 2014
17	Chennamaneni Vidyasagar Rao	30th Aug. 2014	04th Sep. 2019
18	Bhagat Singh Koshyari	05th Sep. 2019	Incumbent

Chief Ministers of Maharashtra

Chief Minister	Tenure
1. Yashwantrao Chavan	From 1st May 1960 to 19th November 1962
2. Marotrao Kannamwar	From 20th November 1962 to 24th November 1963

3. P. K. Sawant	From 25th November 1963 to 4th December 1963
4. Vasantrao Naik	From 5th December 1963 to 1st March 1967
5. Shankarrao Chavan	From 21st February 1975 to 16th May 1977
6. Vasantdada Patil	From 17th May 1977 to 5th March 1978, 5th March 1978 to 18th July 1978
7. Sharad Pawar	From 18th July 1978 to 17th February 1980
8. Abdul Rehman Antulay	From 9th June 1980 to 12th January 1982
9. Babasaheb Bhosale	From 21th January 1982 to 1st February 1983
10. Vasantdada Patil	From 2nd February 1983 to 1st June 1985
11. Shivajirao Patil Nilangekar	From 3rd June 1985 to 6th March 1986
12. Shankarrao Chavan	From 12th March 1986 to 26th June 1988
13. Sharad Pawar	From 26th June 1988 to 3rd March 1990, From 4th March 1990 to 25th June 1991
14. Sudhakarrao Naik	From 25th June 1991 to 22nd February 1993
15. Sharad Pawar	From 6th March 1993 to 14th March 1995
16. Manohar Joshi	From 14th March 1995 to 31st January 1999
17. Narayan Rane	From 1st February 1999 to 17th October 1999
18. Vilasrao Deshmukh	From 18th October 1999 to 16th January 2003
19. Sushilkumar Shinde	From 18th January 2003 to 30th October 2004
20. Vilasrao Deshmukh	From 1st November 2004 to 4th December 2008
21. Ashok Chavan	From 7th November 2009 to 9th November 2010
22. Prithviraj Chavan	From 11th November 2010 to 26th September 2014
23. Devendra Fadnavis	From 31st October 2014 to 12th November 2019
24. Devendra Fadnavis	From 23rd November 2019 to 26th November 2019
25. Uddhav Thackeray	From 28th November 2019

2.2.3 Council of Ministers :

(1) Appointment :

- According to Article 164, Governor appoints the Chief Minister and later the Chief Minister recommends the Governor on the appointment of ministers.
- Ministers shall hold office during the pleasure of the Governor. However in the states of Chhattisgarh, Jharkhand, Madhya Pradesh and Odisha, Governor also appoints a tribal affairs minister.
- The strength of the State Council of Ministers cannot be more than 15% of the strength of State Legislative Assembly. And not less than 12 ministers.
- The State Council of Ministers is collectively responsible before the State Legislative Assembly. Salary and allowances of ministers are determined by state legislature from time to time .

(2) Composition :

- Like at the Centre, in the states too, the council of ministers consists of three categories of ministers, namely, cabinet ministers, ministers of state, and deputy ministers.
- The difference between them lies in their respective ranks, emoluments, and political importance. At the top of all these ministers stands the chief minister the supreme governing authority in the state

Cabinet Ministers :

- Cabinet Ministers are those ministers who are given cabinet rank. They hold independent charge of the important departments like finance, Local Bodies, home affairs, health etc.
- They together determine the policies of the state. The CM and the cabinet ministers together constitute the State Cabinet. It is the most powerful part of the State Council of Ministers.
- It is the highest decision-making authority in the administrative system of a state.
- It is the chief policy formulating body of the state government.
- It is the supreme executive authority of the state government.
- It is an advisory body to the governor.

- It is the chief crisis manager and thus deals with all emergency situations.
- It deals with all major legislative and financial matters.

The ministers of state :

- They can either be given independent charge of departments or can be attached to cabinet ministers. However, they are not members of the cabinet and do not attend the cabinet meetings unless specially invited when something related to their departments is considered by the cabinet.

The deputy ministers :

- They are not given independent charge of departments. They are attached to the cabinet ministers and assist them in their administrative, political and parliamentary duties. They are not members of the cabinet and do not attend cabinet meetings.

(3) Powers, Function and Role :

- According to Article 163,there shall be a Council of Ministers to aid and advise the Governor in the exercise of his functions, except in so far as he is required to exercise his functions in his discretion. According to Article 166, all executive action of the Government of a State shall be expressed to be taken in the name of the Governor. The Governor shall make rules for the more convenient transaction of the business of the government of the state, and for the allocation among ministers of the said business in so far as it is not business with respect to which the Governor is required to act in his discretion.

Advocate-General for the State : Article 165, the Governor of each State shall appoint a person who is qualified to be appointed a Judge of a High Court to be an Advocate-General for the State. It shall be the duty of the Advocate-General to give advice to the Government of the State upon such legal matters, and to perform such other duties of a legal character, as may from time to time be referred or assigned to him by the Governor, and to discharge the functions conferred on him by or under this Constitution or any other law for the time being in force. The Advocate-General shall hold office during the pleasure of the Governor, and shall receive such remuneration as the Governor may determine.

✧ QUESTIONS ✧

Q. I : Answer the following questions in short :

(1) *Write the name of the two former Presidents.*

(2) *Write the names of two former Vice Presidents.*

(3) *Write the Tenure of the President.*

(4) *Write about any five Prime Ministers of India.*

(5) *Write the names of any five Chief Ministers of Maharashtra.*

(6) *Who is included in the Executive Board of India?*

(7) *Write the names of five Indian Prime Ministers.*

(8) *Name two Governors of Maharashtra.*

Q. II : Write short notes on :

(1) *Tenure and the Qualification of the President*

(2) *Tenure and the qualification of the Vice President*

(3) *Attorney General of India*

(4) *Eligibility and Tenure of the Governor*

(5) *Appointment and Tenure of Prime Minister*

(6) *Oath of President*

(7) *Presidential eligibility and tenure*

(8) *Vice-Presidential eligibility and tenure*

(9) *Eligibility and tenure of Governor*

(10) *Appointment and tenure of Chief Minister*

(11) *Presidential Oath*

Q. III :Answer the following questions in 150 to 200 words:

(1) *State the Powers and functions of the President.*

(2) *State the Power and functions of the Vice President.*

(3) *State the Powers and functions of the Prime Minister.*

(4) *State the Structure of council of ministers.*

(5) *Write the powers and functions of the Governor.*

(6) *Write the powers and functions of the Chief Minister.*

(7) *Explain the powers, functions and role of the council of minister of the state.*

(8) *Write the powers, functions and role of the council of general. Federal council of Ministers.*

(9) *Write about the appointment and tenure of the Prime Minister.*

(10) *Write about the structure of the council of ministers.*

(11) *Write in detail about the powers and functions of the Governor.*

(12) *Write in detail about the powers and functions of the Chief Minister.*

(13) *Explain the powers, function and role of the council of ministers.*

Q. IV : Answer the following questions in 500 words (in detail) :

(1) *Write in detail about the executive branch of India.*

(2) *Write in detail about the executive branch of the state in India.*

(3) *Write in detail about Union Executive Board of India.*

(4) *Write in detail about the State Executive Board.*

QUESTIONS FROM PAST UNIVERSITY EXAMINATIONS

Q. 1 : Explain the structure, Rights and Functions of Election Commission of India. **(April 2014, Nov. 2014, April 2016)**

Q. 2. Explain structure of Election Commission of India. **(April 2015, Oct. 2015, 2016, 2017)**

Q. 3. Discuss about the Electoral Reforms in India. **(April 2017)**

***

UNIT – 3

INDIAN JUDICIARY SYSTEM

SYNOPSIS

Introduction :

The essence of a federal constitution is the division of power between a central government and state governments and this division is expressed in written words. Since language is opt to be ambiguous, and its meaning may be not be taken as the same by all at times, it is certain that in any federation there will be disputes between the center and the units about the terms of the division of powers and the respective areas of their authority. All such disputes are settled with reference to the constitution which is the supreme law and which embodies the manner in which powers are divided between the center and the units. Justice demands, at the same time, that such conflict should be settled by an independent and impartial arbiter. A Supreme Court under a Federal Constitution is such an arbiter and is, therefore, an essential part of a federal system. It is at once the highest interpreter of the constituent units. This is one of the most important functions of the Supreme Court of India under the federal system established by the Constitution.

The Supreme Court of India, however, is more than a federal supreme court. Article 32 which is a part of Fundamental Rights that says the court is made the protector of all the fundamental rights embodied in the Constitution. The highly important position that the Court holds under the Constitution was described by a leading member of the Drafting Committee. Alladi Krishnaswami Aiyar, in the following terms:

'The future evolution of the Indian Constitution will thus depend to a large extent upon the work of the Supreme Court and the direction given to it by that Court. From time to time, in the interpretation of the Constitution, the Supreme Court will be confronted with apparently contradictory forces at work in the society for the time being while its functions may be one of interpreting the Constitution... it cannot in the discharge of its duties afford to ignore the social, economic and political tendencies of the times which furnish the necessary background. It has to keep the poise between the seemingly contradictory forces. In the process of the interpretation of the constitution, on certain occasions, it may appear to strengthen the union at the expense of the units and at another it may appear to champion the cause of provincial autonomy and regionalism. On one occasion it may appear to favor individual liberty as against social or state control and at another time it may appear to favour social or state control. It is the great tribunal which has to draw the line between individual liberty and social control.'

A Single Judicial System

Unlike many countries with federal Constitutions, India has a single judicial system. This however, is not an altogether novel feature that has come in with the present constitution. It was there, in a limited sense, under the Constitution Act of 1935, with the Federal Court as the highest court within India in all constitutional matters. But the Federal Court was not the ultimate judicial authority, as appeals could go to the Judicial committee of the privy council in London even from the federal Court.

In India, the highest judicial authority is the Supreme Court. Below the Supreme Court, there exists a High Court in each state. Below the high courts, there exist civil and criminal Courts for each district and there lie the subordinate Courts at the bottom. The

Supreme Court consists of the Chief Justice of India. On 26th January 1950, the Indian Constitution was written and it is the world's largest constitution that is written. The constitution is the source of law in India and also the supreme law of India. Judicial System of India consists of Supreme Court, High Court, District Court or Subordinate Court. The structure of Indian judiciary System is as follow :

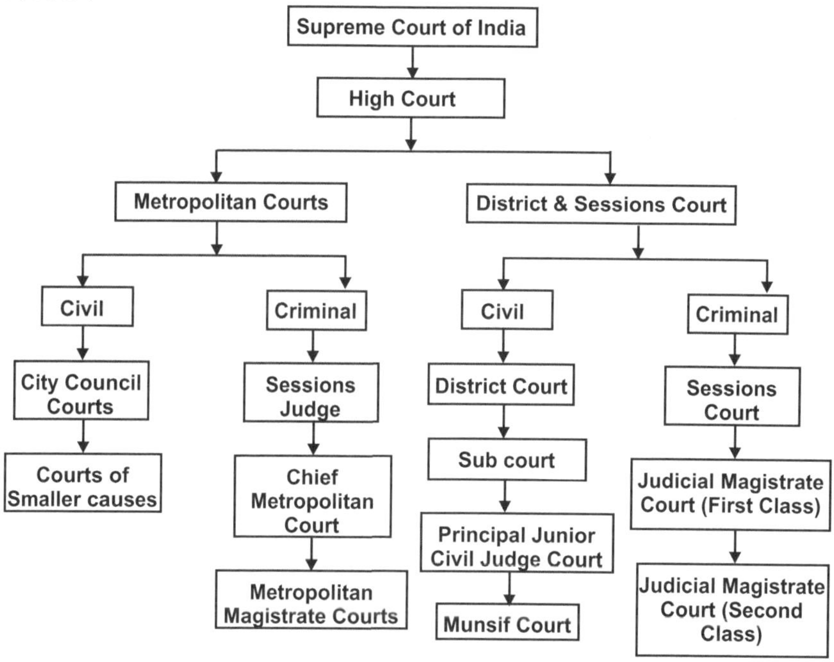

Fig. 3.1 : Structure of Indian Judiciary

3.1 The Supreme Court (Article 124)

The Supreme Court at present consists of the chief justice and 25 other judges. In 1950, when the court was inaugurated with the new Constitution, it had only 8 judges. But a parliamentary enactment in 1957, increased the number to a total of 11. At present, 26 judges including the Chief Justice comprise the Court. **Article 124(1) and Amendment Act of 2008 states that there shall be a Supreme Court of India** consisting of a Chief justice of India (CJI) and **31 judges including the CJI.** Article 124(2) states that every judge of the Supreme Court shall be appointed by the President by warrant under his hand and seal after consultation with such of the judges of Supreme Court and of the High Courts in the states.

Independence of the Supreme Court :

The constitution is conceived as an independent court. Every member in the Constituent assembly had been eager to see that the court was made as independent as it possibly could be. There was a detailed discussion on this very important matter. As a member emphasized:

'This is the institution which will preserve those fundamental rights and secure to every citizen the rights that have been given to him under the constitution. Hence, it must naturally be above all interference by the Executive. The Supreme Court is the watch-dog of democracy.'

The Independence of the judges is ensured by eight main provisions.

(1) Appointment
(2) Qualification
(3) Tenure
(4) Prohibition of practice after retirement
(5) Removal
(6) Remuneration
(7) Establishment
(8) Immunities

(1) Appointment :

- Every judge of the Supreme Court is appointed by the President of India after consultation with such of the judges of the Supreme Court and the High Court of the states as the President may deem necessary for the purpose. But in the appointment of a judge other than the Chief Justice of India by the President is obligatory.
- A special 9 judges Bench of the Court in its unanimous opinion on the Presidential reference held that the Chief Justice of India must make a recommendation to appoint a judge of the

Supreme Court and to transfer a Chief Justice or a puisne judge of a High Court in consultation with the four senior-most puisne judges of the Supreme court. The expression 'consultation with the Chief Justice of India' in article 217(1) and 222(1) of the Constitution requires consultation with a plurality of judges in the formation of the opinion of the Chief justice. It is to be noted in this context that the process of appointment of judges is an integrated participatory consultative process for selecting the best and most suitable persons available and all the constitutional functionaries must perform this duty collectively to reach an agreed decision subserving the constitutional purpose.

- To deal with the appointment and all related matters, a National Judicial Commission was proposed from time to time by the law Ministry and several other authorities. However, so far the proposed National Judicial Commission has not yet been constituted.

(2) Qualifications :

- The elimination of politics in the appointment of judges was further achieved by prescribing high minimum qualifications in the Constitution itself. This is also intended to enhance the competence of those appointed as the judges of the highest court in the country. The qualifications are:
- The person concerned must be a citizen of India
- Either
  (1) is in the opinion of the President a distinguished jurist.
  (2) has been a High Court Judge for at least 5 years; or
  (3) has been for at least 10 years an advocate of a High Court;

(3) Tenure :

- Although the Constitution does not provide for life tenure, the existing provision in effect amounts to nearly the same, as judges once appointed hold office until they complete the age of 65 years. A retiring age of 65 is, by Indian standards, very high, considering the average expectation of life in India and the average fitness of persons for work in old age.

(4) Prohibition of Practice after Retirement :

- A retired judge of the Supreme Court is prohibited from practicing law before any court or authority within the territory of India. But there is no constitutional prohibition against a retired judge being appointed for a specialized form of work by the Government. It was pointed out in the assembly that a retired judge should never be appointed for any office of profit under the government and that they should be placed on the same footing, in this respect, with retired members of the public service Commissions.
- There was no intimate relation between executive and judiciary. In fact, there is complete separation between the function of the two. Consequently, the chances of the Government influencing the conduct of a member of the judiciary are remote. Besides, there are many cases where the employment of judicial talent in a specialized form is necessary for certain purposes, such as conducting enquires, special investigation, etc.

(5) Removal :

- A judge of the Supreme Court can be removed from his position only on the ground of proved misbehaviour or incapacity. Parliament is empowered to regulate the procedure for the investigation and proof of such misbehaviour or incapacity. But whatever be the procedure, each House in order to remove the judge, will have to pass a resolution supported by 2/3 of the members present and a majority of the total membership of the House. Such a resolution will be addressed to the President who will then pass the order of removal of the judge.

(6) Remuneration :

- A very important element that determines the independence of any functionary is the remuneration that he receives as well as its dependence or otherwise on the will of somebody else. With respect to the judges of the Supreme Court, the constitution has taken care of this, unlike many other Constitutions, which leave the fixation of salary to the Legislature. Neither the salary, allowances and privileges nor his rights in respect of leave or absence or pension (to which he is entitled after retirement) can be varied to this disadvantage after his appointment. There is, however, one exception to his almost absolute rule. The salaries of the judges may be reduced by a law of Parliament during a grave financial emergency declared by the president.

(7) Establishment :

- The framers were not content with salary alone. They went a step further and authorized the Supreme Court to have its own establishment and to have complete control over it. In the absence of such a provision they thought that the Courts Independence may become illusory. If the establishment looks for preferment or for promotion to the other quarters, it is likely to sap the independence of the judiciary.

(8) Immunities :

- Finally, the independence of the court is further safeguarded by making all actions and decisions of the judges in their official capacity immune from criticism. This does not mean that no one may object a decision of the court or an opinion of a judge to a critical academic analysis. All that is prohibited is the imputation of movities on the part of the judges in arriving at decisions and action. Even the parliament may not discuss the conduct of a judge except when a resolution for his removal is before it. In order to maintain the dignity of the court and to protect it from malicious and tendentious criticism, it has the power of initiating contempt of court proceedings against any alleged offender and take appropriate action.
- Article 144 states that all authorities civil and judicial in the territory of India shall act in aid of the Supreme Court.

Powers of the Supreme Court

1. **Power to punish for contempt (civil or criminal) of court** with simple imprisonment for 6 months or a fine up to ₹ 2000. Civil contempt means willful disobedience to any judgment. Criminal contempt means doing any act which lowers the authority of the court or causing interference in judicial proceedings

2. **Judicial review** : To examine constitutionality of legislative enactments and executive orders. The grounds of review are limited by- Parliamentary legislation or rules made by Supreme Court.
3. **Deciding authority :** Deciding authority regarding election of President and Vice President.
4. **Enquiring authority :** Enquiring authority in conduct and behaviour of UPSC members.
5. **Withdraw cases pending :** Withdraw cases pending before high courts and dispose them itself.
6. **Appointment of ad hoc judges :** Article 127 states that if at any time there is lack of quorum of Judges of Supreme Court, the CJI may with previous consent of the President and Chief Justice of the High Court concerned request in writing the attendance of Judge of High Court duly qualified to be appointed as a Judge of the SC.
7. **Appointment of Retired Judges of Supreme Court or High Court :** Article 128- The CJI at any time with the previous consent of the President and the person to be so appointed can appoint any person who had previously held office of a Judge of SC.
8. **Appointment of acting Chief Justice :** Article 126 - when the office of CJI is vacant or when the Chief Justice is by reason of absence or otherwise unable to perform duties of office, the President in such a case can appoint a judge of the Court to discharge the duties of office.
9. **Revisory Jurisdiction :** The Supreme Court under Article 137 is empowered to review any judgment or order made by it with a view to removing any mistake or error that might have crept in the judgment or order.
10. **Supreme Court as a Court of Record :** The Supreme Court is a court of record as its decisions are of evidentiary value and cannot be questioned in any court.

3.2 High Court

We have already seen the position of the Supreme Court with the inauguration of the new constitution in 1950, and how it affected the position of the High Courts by bringing them directly under the Supreme Court as parts of a single, integrated, and hierarchical, all India judicial system. The Constitution does not, however, vest in the Supreme Court any direct administrative control over the High Courts which would substantially affect their functioning as independent judicial institutions.

The position of the High Courts under a federal Constitution like that of India is substantially different from the State Courts under most other federations, notably that of the United States of America. There, the State Courts are constituted under the judicial system. The method of appointment and conditions of service of the judges of the State Courts as well as their respective jurisdictions vary from State to state. In India, on the contrary, there is uniformity in all these matters and the Constitution lays down detailed provisions dealing with them. Neither the State Executive nor the State Legislature has any power to control the High Court, or to alter the constitution or organization of the High Court. Whatever that is permissible, short of a constitutional amendment, is vested in parliament. These provisions have great importance in determining the independence of the High Courts.

The High Courts of India are the principal civil courts of original jurisdiction in each state and union territory. However, a high court exercises its original civil and criminal jurisdiction only if the subordinate courts are not authorized by law to try such matters for lack of pecuniary, territorial jurisdiction. High courts may also enjoy original jurisdiction in certain matters, if so designated specifically in a state or federal law.

However, the work of most high courts primarily consists of appeals from lower courts and writ petitions in terms of Article 226 of the constitution. Writ jurisdiction is also an original jurisdiction of a high court. Each state is divided into judicial districts presided over by a district and sessions judge. He is known as a district judge when he presides over a civil case and a session's judge when he presides over a criminal case. He is the highest judicial authority below a high court judge. Below him, there are courts of civil jurisdiction, known by different names in different states. Under Article 141 of the constitution, all courts in India, including high courts, are bounded by the judgments and orders of the Supreme Court of India by precedence.

Judges in a high court are appointed by the President of India in consultation with the Chief Justice of India and the governor of the state. High courts are headed by a chief justice. The chief justices rank fourteenth (within their respective states) and seventeenth (outside their respective states) on the Indian order of precedence. The number of judges in a court is decided by dividing the average institution of main cases during the last five years by the national average, or the average rate of disposal of main cases per judge per year in that High Court, whichever is higher.

The Calcutta High Court is the oldest high court in the country, established on 2 July 1862. High courts that handle numerous cases of a particular region have permanent benches established there. Benches are also present in states which come under the jurisdiction of a court outside its territorial limits. Smaller states with few cases may have circuit benches established. Circuit benches (known as circuit courts in some parts of the world) are temporary courts which hold proceedings for a few selected months in a year. Thus, cases built up during this interim period are judged when the circuit court is in session.

- According to a study conducted by a Bangalore-based NGO, Daksh, on 21 high courts in collaboration with the Ministry of Law and Justice in March 2015, it was found that average pendency of a case in high courts in India is 3 years. High Courts look after the issues which are not solved in a district Court. High Courts were first established in three presidency cities of Calcutta, Bombay and Madras in 1862. The high court of Delhi came up in 1966.

- Currently, there are 21 high courts. While many states have their own high courts, Punjab and Haryana share a common high court at Chandigarh, and seven northeast states have a common high court at Guwahati. Some high courts have been benches in other parts of the state for greater accessibility.

Appointment of Judges :

Differing legal perceptions on the scope and content of the consultation process between the Executive and the Chief Justice of the Supreme court led to the President referring the matter to the Supreme Court for its opinion in 1998. The Court held that the expression "Consultation with the chief Justice of India" in Articles 217(1) and 222(1) of the Constitution requires consultation with a plurality of judges in the formation of the opinion of the Chief justice, plurality here means two senior-most judges of the Supreme Court. In the case of transfer of High Court judges, the Court held that the recommendation should be made by the Chief Justice in consultation with four senior most judges of the Supreme Court.

Qualification :

The minimum qualifications prescribed for appointment are Indian citizenship and at least 10 years 'experience either as an advocate of a High Court in India or as a judicial officer in the territory of India.' In computing the 10 year period for the purpose of appointment, experience as an advocate can be combined with that of a judicial officer. A judge of the High Court can be removed from office only for proved misbehaviour or incapacity and only in the same manner in which a judge of the Supreme Court is removed.

Jurisdiction :

The Constitution does not attempt detailed definitions and classification of the different types of jurisdiction of the High Court as it has done in the case of the Supreme Court. This is mainly because most of the High Courts at the time of the framing of the Constitution had been functioning with well-defined jurisdictions, whereas the Supreme Court was a newly-created institution necessitating a clear definition of its powers and functions. Moreover, the High Courts were expected to maintain the same position that they originally had as the highest court in the state even after the inauguration of the Constitution.

Apart from the normal original and appellate jurisdiction, the Constitution also vests four additional powers in the High Courts.

These are :

(1) The power to issue writs or orders for the enforcement of the Fundamental Rights or for any other purpose;

(2) The power of superintendence over all Courts in the State.

(3) The power to transfer cases to itself from subordinate Courts concerning the interpretation of the constitution and

(4) The power to appoint officers and servants of the High Court.

3.3 Judicial Review

Over a century and a half ago, the Supreme Court of the United States made a famous pronouncement of far-reaching importance. It was in the course of its judgment in the famous case of Marbury vs. Madison. The judge who spoke for the unanimous Court was the great John Marshall, chief justice of the United States. Marshall said:

'...certainly all those who have framed written constitutions contemplate them as forming the fundamental and paramount law of the nation, and consequently, the theory of every such Government must be that an act of the Legislature, repugnant to the constitution, is void.'

On the strength of this theory, the court declared a congressional enactment invalid and thereby firmly established the doctrine of judicial review.

Under the Constitution of India, Parliament is not supreme. Its powers are limited in two ways. First there is division of power between the union and the state. Parliament is competent to pass laws only with respect to those subjects which are guaranteed to the citizen against very form of legislative encroachment. Being the guardian of the Fundamental Rights and the arbiter of powers between them, the Supreme Court stands in a unique position wherefrom it is competent to exercise the power of reviewing legislative enactments both of Parliament and the State Legislatures. This is what makes the court a powerful instrument of judicial review under the Constitution.

The Keshavanand Bharati decision is indeed a watershed in the annals of judicial performance. It is the most important so far from the point of view of its far-reaching effect. By that decision the Court struck down a constitutional amendment on the ground that it violated the basic structure or framework of the Constitutional amendment. The concept of basic structure is creative and innovative interpretation of the Constitution. The court has, however, not spelt out as to what it means by basic structure of the Constitution or a list of its basic features, but has reserved its right to declare these as and when the situation arises.

3.4 Judicial Activism

Judicial Activism has not been a spontaneous development. It is the consequence of a situation which necessitated it. In 1985, the then Chief Justice of India, Justice P. Bhagvati converted a letter written to him on a post card by an aggrieved person into public interest litigation (PIL). That was the beginning of judicial activism. By the middle of the 90's the court's role in this field became well understood and widely appreciated.

- The Court's role in sensitizing the Central Intelligence Agencies to discharge their constitutional obligations in the hawala cases in which top leaders both in the Government and in the Opposition were involved, its various judgments ranging from the need to have a uniform civil code, pollution control, preservation of historical monuments, cleaning and keeping the metropolises more hygienic, directing the eviction of unauthorized occupation of government building, in camera trial victims and the award of compensation to them, punishing senior civil servants for contempt, prohibiting children employed in hazardous industries, directing the closure of all acqua farms in coastal areas and a host of such other decisions have attracted both praise and criticism.

✧ QUESTIONS ✧

Q. I : Answer the following questions in short :

(1) *At present how many Chief Justice are there in the Supreme Court?*

(2) *When was the Supreme Court established in India?*

(3) *Which three High Courts were first established in India ?*

(4) *At present, how many High Courts are there in India ?*

(5) *Write any two names of Chief Justice of the Supreme Court.*

(6) *What is Judicial Review ?*

(7) *What is judicial Activism.*

(8) *Who appoints the Chief Justice of Supreme Court ?*

(9) *Who appoints the Chief Justice of High Courts ?*

(10) *Which are the additional powers vested in the High Courts ?*

Q. II : Write short notes on :

(1) *Appointment of judges in the Supreme Court.*

(2) *Appointment of judges in the High Court.*

(3) *Duration of chief justice of Supreme Court.*

(4) *Duration of Chief Justice of High Court.*

(5) *Appointment of judges of Supreme Court.*

(7) *Independences of the judges of Supreme Court.*

Q. III : Answer the following questions in 150 to 200 words :

(1) *Explain the concept of Judicial Review.*

(2) *Explain the concept of Judicial Activism.*

(3) *Discuss the Prohibition of Practice after retirement of the judge of Supreme Court.*

(4) *Discuss the powers of the supreme court.*

(5) *Explain the independence of the Supreme Court.*

(6) *Qualification and jurisdiction of the High Court.*

Q. IV : Answer the following questions in 500 words : (in detail)

(1) Explain the independences of Judges (eight provisions) of Supreme Court.

(2) State the Composition of High Court. State its powers and responsibilities.

QUESTIONS FROM PREVIOUS EXAMINATIONS

(1) Write the structure, of Powers and functions of Supreme Court. **(April 2014)**

(2) Write the Composition, Power and Functions of High Court. **(April 2015, 16, Oct. 2016)**

(3) Judicial Activism. **(April 2015, 2017, 2018)**

(4) Judicial Review and Judicial Activism. **(April 2016)**

❋ ❋ ❋

UNIT – 4

ELECTORAL SYSTEMS

SYNOPSIS

4.1 Election Commission : Composition, Functions and Role

4.1.1 Electoral System in India

- The Election Commission is a permanent and independent body established and empowered by the constitution of India. The Election Commission of India was established to ensure free and fair elections in the country. It is an independent body having the power of superintendence, direction and control of elections of the world's largest democracy and it is kept away by the Indian constitution makers from political interference.

(1) Background of the Election Commission :

The provision was made in Morley-Minto reforms of 1909 to conduct elections by an independent body. A voting rights committee was formed by the commission of 1928 and in 1931 under the presidency of Lord Lethian, to conduct general elections of the country in a fearless and impartial environment the makers of the Indian Constitution created an independent and capable Election Commission of India.

(2) Composition of the Election Commission :

Article 324 to 328 of the Indian Constitution provides that the power of superintendence, direction and control of elections to Parliament, State legislatures, The office of the President of India and office of Vice President of India shall be vested in the election commission. The election commission of India is considered one of the four pillars of the constitution. The election commission is solely responsible for conduction of elections in India. Since its Inception in 1950 and till 15th October 1989, the election commission functioned as a single member body consisting of the chief election commissioner. Now, there are two other commissioners who are being appointed after reforms.

Eligibility :

The following criteria are necessary to be appointed as Election Commissioner

- He should be a citizen of India.
- He should satisfy all the conditions determined by the commission.
- He should have administrative experience.

Appointment :

- The election commissioner is appointed by the President of India. The chief election commissioner receives. Salary, allowances and other perquisites which are similar to those of a judge of a Supreme Court. The tenure is fixed at completion of 6 years or 65 years of age whichever is earlier. The power to determine the condition of service and tenure is vested with the office of the President and the parliament.

Impeachment :

The process of impeachment to remove the election commissioner from his post is same as that of the impeachment process of a judge of a Supreme Court.

Other Staff :

- Election Commission of India has a chief election commissioner and two other election commissioners. The election commission is assisted by Deputy Election Commissioners. They are drawn from the civil service and appointed by the commission with tenure system. They are assisted, in turn, by the secretary as joint secretary as deputy secretary and under secretaries posted in the secretariat of the commission. The office of the commission is known as the secretariat of the election commission.
- For the execution and conduction of election duties the commission draws employees from the central and state government services on the basis of deputation.

System :

- The election commission is a capable organization for planning and execution of elections. The system is controlled by the centre to States and States to district level to constituency. The election commission gets work done by engaging various officials of different levels.

4.1.2 Power and Functions of the Election Commission :

The composition of the Indian election commission is unique. Many constitutions in the world have no provision of an independent Election Commission. That responsibility is vested in the legislature itself. In India, the election commission has many functions. Holding elections of the world's largest democracy having more than 60 crores of voters which includes the elections to the parliament, legislative assemblies of different states, office of the President, vice president and other important elections in the country ensuring organisation and execution impartially. No person or institution can interfere with the functions of the election commission. The constitution has provided some special powers to the election commission due to which its significance is still protected.

Voter's list :

To prepare periodically revised electoral rolls and to register all eligible voters above 18 years of age irrespective of their caste, religion, race, gender etc.

Conduction of the elections :

- To determine the territorial areas of the electoral constituencies throughout the country on the basis of delimitation commission act of parliament. It also includes :
- To grant recognition to the regional and national parties.
- To notify the dates and schedules of elections.
- Appointment of necessary officers for the execution of work, their training and equipment with necessary material.
- Allotment of election symbols to the parties, scrutinize nomination papers and to determine the model code of conduct for the election to be observed by the parties during elections.

Election results :

Counting votes after general elections, declaring date and time and declaring results of the election and providing certificates to the elected candidates.

By-election :

The election commission has made it mandatory to held elections in case of vacation of the office of Lok Sabha MP or MLA due to death or any other reasons within six months. But it's not binding if the tenure of the Lok Sabha or State legislative assembly is remaining less than six months.

Cancellation of election :

- To cancel polls in the event of rigging, booth capturing, violence and other irregularities. Election Commission holds power to disqualify a person from the public office if proven guilty of malpractices during elections.

4.1.3 Election Process :

The electoral process is determined according to the provisions of the election commission. The commission has power to declare elections they are planning for their postponement. The electoral process is very important for the democracy and it is the responsibility of the election commission to execute the electoral process fairly and impartially.

(1) **Election Notification :** The election commission notifies the dates and schedules of the elections. It determines the time period to file nominations and to withdraw nominations. It is mandatory for the candidates to file nominations or withdraw nominations in a given period. The campaigning period is allotted to the political parties and candidates.

(2) **Nomination and Deposit :** The nomination and the deposit amount determined by the commission should be submitted. Candidate is expected to provide valid information including name, address, property details, cases filed in his name etc. The commission has described ₹ 10,000 as deposit amount for open category for Lok Sabha elections and deposit amount of the SC and ST category have half deposit amount of the previous.

(3) **Voting, Votes Counting and Results :** According to the directions of the election commission, election booths are setup in every constituency in the country. Necessary facilities are provided on the election booths. On every voting centre a presiding officer is appointed and to assist him other officers and employees are appointed.

- After voting is finished, the process of vote counting is done in a specified period. Political parties candidates or their representatives are allowed to be present at the counting center. If any malpractices are found at any voting centre, there's a provision for re-poll or postponement of voting.

(4) **Important Changes in the Election System :** Printed ballot papers were being used since 1952 on which voters could mark their votes by a rubber stamp. This process was very time consuming and costly. The election commission ended this system and introduced electronic voting machines (EVMs) for the elections. It's being used since 2004 in general elections. It made the voting process easy and more efficient. Also, it reduced the expenses of paper and other stationery. After 2014 general elections few political parties and candidates opposed EVMs but in the era of modern technology the steps are proving beneficial.

4.2 Chief Election Commissioner

The chief Election Commissioner is one of the most important posts in India along with Chief Justice of the Supreme Court and Comptroller and Auditor General of India. The post of the chief election commissioner of India came into existence on 21st March 1950 and Sukumar Sen was the first chief election Commissioner. Later the demand for the expansion of the commission was raised. Joint members committee of 1972 recommended that. Opposition made similar demands in 1975. The then Prime Minister Rajiv Gandhi recommended the expansion of the commission into a multi member body which was granted by the President. Since 1993 the election commission functions as a multi member body having a Chief election Commissioner and two other commissioners.

If we briefly look at the service and the tenure of the Chief Election Commissioners, first Chief election Commissioner Sukumar Sen and second K. V. Sundaram have served for very long period that's 10 years each. Many persons served as the election commissioner but late T. N. Seshan who held the post from 12th December 1990 gave dignity to the office during his tenure and the electoral reforms he brought. Many decisions and reforms made by Mr. Seshan became responsible for the conflicts with many politicians.

It was discussed by the media, political parties and political experts that the commission be made a three member body to check the power of Mr. Seshan. T. N. Seshan introduced the photo identity card for the voters. Apart from curtailing bogus voting; it helped Seshan reach the common people. Later, that card began to be used as ID proof to avail many government schemes. This voter ID card was issued during the tenure of T. N. Seshan hence it was also called as Seshan card. Currently Mr. Sunil Arora is serving as chief election commissioner of India since 2nd December 2018.

4.3 Electoral Reforms in India

India is the world's largest democracy. Since 1950, issues like election, election process, and electoral reforms are constantly discussed. An electoral Reforms Commission was appointed under the leadership of justice V. M. Tarkunde. The legal age for voting was determined as 21 years, later to involve youth in the democratic process it was changed to 18 years during the tenure of the then Prime Minister Rajiv Gandhi.

4.3.1 Changes in the Election Process :

1. **Voters Age :** Voting age was changed from 21 years to 18 years
2. **Campaign period :** Since 1996 the campaign period is determined between the last day of withdrawal of nomination to the first day of voting which is for 14 days.

- Filing nominations for more than two constituencies by the same person is prohibited.

3. **Restrictions on the Citizens :** To maintain the law and order possession of arms is prohibited. Police force is excluded from this.
4. **Voters List :** Recognised political parties of the country get a voters list by the commission which free of cost.
5. **By-election :** The election commission has made it mandatory to hold elections incase of vacation of the office of Lok Sabha MP or MLA due to death or any other reasons within six months. But it's not binding if the tenure of the Lok Sabha or State legislative assembly is remaining less than six months.
6. **Public Holiday :** To ensure the maximum participation of the voters and to ensure that no person is deprived of his right to vote a public holiday is declared for all the employees working in the public or private sector. Members of the armed forces and officers employees on election duty are provided with the facility to cast their votes through posts.

7. **Election Officials :** An election duty is a national duty therefore according to the 1998 act, performing election duty is mandatory for the officials working in central, state or state related government services.
8. **Anti-defection Law :** Apart from the electoral reforms to check the behaviour of the elected representatives the Anti-defection law has been passed. Due to this law, switching political parties for personal gains is made difficult.
9. **Election Expenditure :** The election commission has prescribed and controlled the expenditure for the Lok Sabha and State legislative assembly elections. Candidate is bound to submit the details of the expenditure.
10. **Use of Electronic system :** The election commission has introduced electronic voting machines (EVMs). Initially, they were used on experimental basis. Since 2004, it was made compulsory to use EVMs in Lok Sabha and State legislative assembly elections. There is a provision of recording votes for 16 candidates in the machine; if candidates are more than 16, then one more machine is attached. Since 2019, the VVPAT machine is also being used along with EVMs with the help of which, voters can verify to whom they casted their votes to. Because of this electronic system; voting and votes counting process became fast. Also there is reduction in the expenses of paper, transportation, printing and stationery etc.
11. **Model Code of Conduct for Elections :** Since the declaration of notification of election, political parties, candidates and government officials have to follow the model code of conduct prepared by the commission. Any speech, writing or practice that disrupts communal harmony is strictly prohibited. Use of religious places for the election campaign is banned.
12. **Facility for the Voters :** The commission had provided the facility to register the voters and make any changes regarding name or address in the voter's list. Apart from that, voters can check their names in the voters list on the given website.

13. **Changes in the Election Process to the Office of the President and Vice President :** Significant changes have been made in the process of the elections to the office of the President and vice President. Number of nominators for a candidate is changed from 10 to 50 for the presidential candidate and 5 to 20 for the vice presidential candidate.

14. **The State Election Commission :** The state election commission of Maharashtra was established on 26th April 1994. To reduce the workload of the election commission of India, the state election commissions are established. State election commissions are created according to the 73rd and 74th Constitutional Amendment act. The main function of the state election commission is to conduct and administer the elections of the local governing bodies and follow the instructions of the election commission of India. The state election commission is expected to prepare and revise the electoral roll as per the instructions of the election commission of India.

4.3.2 Evaluation of the Performance of the Election Commission

If we briefly review the functioning of the election commission since 1950, we can see the significant changes in their work. The significant changes and effective functioning of the election commission is the outcome of independence, powers and composition of the election commission given by the Constitution. Different reforms have been introduced in the functioning of election commission and according to the changing nature the commission has acquired the use of modern technology which resulted in the catalysed functioning of the commission. Conduction and execution of the elections of the world's largest democracy is a vast and difficult task but the election commission is functioning effectively with the help of civil servants of the country. Code of conduct of the commission is respected by all the spheres of the society.

Chart No. 4.1 : Important Articles about Electoral System

Articles	Part 15 Elections
324	Superintendence, direction and control of elections to be vested in an Election Commission.
325	No person to be ineligible for inclusion in, or to claim to be included in a special, electoral roll on grounds of religion, race, caste or sex.
326	Elections to the House of the People and to the Legislative Assemblies of States to be on the basis of adult suffrage.
327	Power of Parliament to make provisions with respect to elections to Legislatures.
328	Power of Legislature of a State to make provisions with respect to elections to such Legislature.
329	Bar to interference by courts in electoral matters.
329 A	[Repealed.]

✧ QUESTIONS ✧

Q. I : Answer the following questions in short :

(1) *Write any one Article about Electoral System mentioned in the Indian Constitution.*

(2) *Write two names of Chief Election Commissioners of India.*

(3) *What is a Voter List?*

(4) *What is By-Election?*

Q. II : Write short notes on :

(1) *EVM (Electronic Voting Machine)*

(2) *Eligibility for Election Commissioner*

(3) *Election Notification*

(4) *Appointment of Election Commissioner*

(5) *Changes in Electoral Process*

Q. III : Answer the following questions in 150 to 200 words:

(1) *Write the composition of the Election Commission.*

(2) *Write the powers and functions of the Election Commission.*

(3) *Write in detail information about the Chief Election Commissioner.*

(4) *Evaluate the functions and performance of the Election Commissioner.*

Q. IV : Answer the following questions in 500 words (in detail) :

(1) *Describe the composition and the significance and write functions and role of the Election Commission.*

(2) *Explain electoral reforms in the Indian electoral process.*

QUESTIONS FROM PAST UNIVERSITY EXAMINATIONS

Q. 1 : State the Composition, Functions and Role of Election Commission. **(April 2014, Nov. 2014, April 2016)**

Q. 2 : Composition of Election Commission. **(April 2015, Oct. 2015, 2016, 2017)**

Q. 3. State the electoral reforms in India. **(April 2017)**

Q. 4. Performance of the Election Commission. **(Oct. 17)**

✲ ✲ ✲

MODEL QUESTION PAPER

Time : 2 ½ Hours **Marks 70**

Q. I : Answer the following questions in short : (Any Eight) **[16]**

(1) *What is EVM ?*

(2) *Under which Article of the Constitution the Parliament of India constituted ?*

(3) *Write the name of the two former Presidents.*

(4) *Write the names of five former Indian Prime Ministers.*

(5) *Name two former Governors of Maharashtra.*

(6) *Write any two names of Chief Justice of the Supreme Court.*

(7) *What is Judicial Review ?*

(8) *What is judicial Activism ?*

(9) *What is a Voter List?*

(10) *What is By-Election?*

Q. II : Write Short Notes on : (Any Four) **[16]**

(1) Lok Sabha

(2) Oath of President

(3) Attorney General of India

(4) Speaker and Deputy Speaker of an Assembly

(5) Rajya Sabha

Q. III : Answer the following questions in 150 to 200 words : (Any Three) **[18]**

(1) Write the composition of Election Commission of India.

(2) Explain the concept of Judicial Review.

(3) State the Composition of Legislative council.

(4) Explain the Powers and Functions of Election Commission.

Q. IV : Answer the following questions in 500 words : (Any Two) **[20]**

(1) Explain the Powers and Functions of the Parliament.

(2) Explain the Composition of High Court. State its powers.

(3) Explain the Electoral Reforms in India.

❋ ❋ ❋